C000049873

0 3 NOV 2007

SPECIAL HOUSES

SPECIAL HOUSES

Pauline Morgan

Book Guild Publishing
Sussex, England

First published in Great Britain in 2006 by
The Book Guild Ltd
Pavilion View
19 New Road
Brighton
BN1 1UF

Typesetting in Times by
Keyboard Services, Luton, Bedfordshire

Printed in Great Britain by
CPI Bath

A catalogue record for this book is available from
The British Library

ISBN 1 84624 070 0

Contents

Preface

I have been asked so many times, can anybody do what you do? The answer is yes. Situations like this spurred me on to write a book about my spiritual pathway. The only way I could recall my spiritual experiences was to connect them to the houses that I have lived in. I hope that by explaining my personal spiritual experiences, others can relate to them and realise that they too have a special gift.

I use my special gift to assist people who may need advice or are seeking contact with the spirit world. I never accept praise for my work because I have wonderful guardian angels and various spirit guides whom I work with and it is they who do all the hard work, not me! I am merely an instrument to play a wonderful tune on.

My sincere wishes
Pauline Morgan

1

Introduction

I always felt that I was very *special*. However, in what way I did not know. Now in my late forties I realise just how *special* I really am! Being born with such an amazing gift is really wonderful. Nurturing and self-developing the gift throughout my life-path has always brought great pleasure to me. I focused this book on houses that I have lived in, including my present home. This is how I can recall all my psychic experiences – by associating situations to each property. It was in my early thirties that I had the good fortune to meet a local clairvoyant/medium. She told me I had a great gift of second sight and that I should be using it. This made me more aware of who I really was: not *just* a wife or mother! However, the signs have always been there since day one, but some I ignored, much to my cost, as you will see later on in the book. I have decided to change a few names to protect the innocent. I propose to start my book by introducing my family, then proceed to the special houses. Sit comfortably and enjoy how one three-year-old's life has changed by acknowledging the spirits of those who have passed over.

2

The Ferris Family

My family consisted of Bernard Ferris (my father), who came from Belfast in Northern Ireland, and Kathleen Veronica McHugh (my mother), who was born in a small village called Laghy in County Donegal but moved to Londonderry at a very young age. Both parents came from very traditional but strict Roman Catholic families.

My father was one of six children, four boys and two girls. His parents had high standards, which focused on their children being guided into a good standard of education or learning a good trade. Bernard's background was one of a good education, because he was fortunate to have attended the Christian Brothers' School. This school was renowned for being very strict. Everyone who attended always came away with an excellent education. Also, it was seen as a good status symbol for a family to have a son enrolled at such an establishment because it was one of the top grammar schools. The school only took boys, not girls. Bernard enjoyed learning and always had his head in books, but he also had a sense of adventure so he joined the Royal Navy. However, he did lie about his age and forged the signatures of his parents on the consent form. This came to light and my father eventually enrolled at the correct age and signed up for twenty-five years of service. He started life in the Royal Navy as an Able Seaman, and progressed to a Rating Petty Officer. Over a period of time he received numerous medals for service in many countries, including the Burma Star and the Malta Star, to name only two.

My mother had a different family background from that of my father. It was one of sadness because her mother had passed away when she was only a few months old and her father could not cope with bringing up a young family, so the children were divided between various aunts and uncles. The family was never to be reunited all together at the same time, which was sad for my mother because it was her dream to have a family reunion one day. Kathleen was brought up in the Waterside, Londonderry, by an aunt and uncle called Alice and Jack Willoughby. The Willoughby children instantly became Kathleen's brothers and sister. She left school at the tender age of fourteen and started work at Tilley and Henderson's shirt factory, which was renowned for the shirts it produced. However, the employees called it the 'sweat-box' because of the poor working conditions. It was at this establishment my mother found out she had a psychic gift. An older woman who worked in the factory took the young Kathleen under her wing and introduced her to reading the playing cards. This proved to be the chosen pathway for Kathleen, because at a younger age she too had had many strange experiences.

She began to realise just how gifted and talented she really was. Other people got to hear how accurate Kathleen's predictions were and news spread like wildfire throughout the factory. Other people began to recognise Kathleen's psychic ability. I recall the story that my mother told me of how two other girls and a young man went to 'have their fortune told' as they referred to it in those days. The two girls went in first and all was well, then the young man came out explaining that the woman already knew he wore a uniform and worked under the government crown, which was true – he was a policeman. When it came to my mother's turn the woman refused to read for Kathleen because she already sensed that

4

my mother dealt with the cards. To this day history does repeat itself, for when I go to have a personal reading, the same thing happens to me!

Kathleen worked long hours at the factory and conditions were not good but she found her freedom in music and dance. Dancing brought her joy and happiness as she listened to the big band sounds such as the Glenn Miller Band, etc. She was envied because she had natural rhythm as a dancer. She loved to enter local dance competitions at the local British Legion.

My father met my mother while he was stationed with the Royal Navy at the Sea Eagle Barracks, in the Waterside. One evening my father and his friends decided to go into town and as they were passing a group of young women (Kathleen included), Bernard turned around to one of his friends and commented about the lovely little dark-haired woman in the group. He then proceeded to comment that one day he would marry her. His prediction came true. Even then, psychic energies were working together to bring my parents close together. They proceeded to get married and lived in Derry. First they lived in married quarters and then moved on to a local housing estate called the Creggan Estate. Not long after their marriage my mother gave birth to a daughter called Carol. One year and ten months later another child was born – a baby boy named John.

The family decided to move to 108 Arbow Drive in Lurgan, County Armagh, where my father's parents had decided to get away from the bustle of city life in Belfast and seek a slower pace of life. The Ferris family started to increase further with another birth: my older sister Eileen.

Four years later I was born on Friday 13 April 1956 at exactly 6 p.m. (I am the only one in the entire family who knows the town where I was conceived and the actual time of my birth.) I was named Pauline Mary Ferris, and Elizabeth was added later at my confirmation ceremony. My mother would always recall the moment I was born because our

5

family doctor, Dr McCaffery, paid a lovely compliment to me, which was, 'What a beautiful pink baby.' (Here I am now, covered from head to toe in freckles, which are the sign of beauty, or so I'm told!) It was noticed at the home birth that I had a little pink birthmark at the centre of my forehead. My mum was told that it would eventually fade away, but forty-seven years later it is still there, but I see it in a different light! Is it a sign that I had other past lives? Perhaps born into an Eastern religious sect, or had I been shot in the forehead for some unknown reason? I know that I am *special* but in what way? All will be revealed later!

About five years later, another daughter was born, named Orla. During Orla's early years she was not a strong child because she had suspected tuberculosis, perhaps as a result of, so the doctors said, consuming unpasteurised milk. This meant that the family had to undergo a lot of tests and X-rays. Luckily it was not as serious as originally suspected. The family would have consisted of eight children in total, but one daughter were classed as a stillborn. Then shortly afterwards my mother had a further two miscarriages.

3

The Lurgan Tarry

After serving twenty-five years in the Royal Navy, my father decided that the family should move back to Lurgan. This town could only be portrayed as a thriving market town where textiles such as linen were produced in abundance and other industries such as clothing kept the growing the population employed. Lurgan came under the civil parish of Shankill and had its own church and clergyman. The town is positioned close to the south-eastern shores of Lough Neagh, in County Armagh, Northern Ireland. It is situated approximately twenty-five miles to the west of Belfast and ninety-five miles north of Dublin. The nearest town is Portadown, which is six miles to the west.

Lurgan derives from the Gaelic name 'An lorgain', meaning a long, low ridge of land. It has a famous saying: 'Your face is as long as the Lurgan spade.' In other words, if you're in a mood and this shows in your facial expression, then you are compared to a long, slim-bladed spade.

The centre of the town has changed over the years. For example, the main street in Victorian times was lined with four rows of various types of property. Today no one would ever know about the middle row of properties because a huge, wide road has replaced the Victorian buildings that once stood there.

When we left Lurgan the family gave up their rights to a council home. This meant they would have to start all over again by putting their name on a list and going through the general procedures. My father's parents suggested that the family should stay with them until a suitable property was found. My grandparents moved from the hustle and bustle of Belfast to a much slower pace of living in Lurgan. The Lurgan Tarry was an area just beyond the housing estates and bordering the countryside. My grandparents' house was one of a pair of semi-detached labourers' cottages and their neighbours where called Mary and Jim Marley. Mr and Mrs Marley had a huge family of about twelve children: two girls and the rest boys. Some did not survive, but traditional Catholics at that time did tend to have big families whereas today even Catholics tend to have only one or two. The Marley residence was no bigger than my grandparents' home. However, my grandparents' property was quite big, or maybe it *seemed* like that looking through the eyes of a two-and-a-half-year-old.

The house was set in about a quarter of an acre and had an orchard and a well that was still functional. I always remember the feeling of not wanting to be alone where the outside toilet was because you had to go into a big shed and the toilet was in a very dark corner of the shed. The whole shed area had a creepy feel to it, and I used to hear people whispering. When I called out the whispering would stop!

The house itself had a particular smell of home baking (soda and potato bread) and Manson furniture polish, because my Granny used to work as a young parlour maid for one of the big houses in Belfast before she married my Granddad and was always renowned for keeping a good home.

The Lurgan Tarry had many unexplained entities and strange stories of weird happenings that would connect to both houses. Mrs Marley always felt that the previous householder had not fully passed over to the spirit world because the younger members of the Marley family would talk about the various sightings of strangers who would visit the home. Even though there may have been five people actually in my Granny's living room, it *felt* as if the room was crowded. I always sensed strange happenings attached to this property such as objects falling off the shelves or pictures falling to the ground. No one would be near any of these items when they fell and I would sometimes get the blame! In fact, I was definitely *not* near them. I always recall my Granny saying 'that's so and so's fault'; she would give the entities names but was never put out by these strange happenings.

My grandparents always appeared to be old-looking, but then again that was how children always perceived their elders. I was never frightened of my grandparents but as children we where always taught to respect our elders. On the other hand, Granddad always made the children laugh with the funny faces he would pull. Granny was more serious about life in general and we would not fool around her because she would tell us off. We always had a warning from our mother to be on our best behaviour. When I got to my late teens, I developed a better relationship with her, and could talk about boyfriends, etc.

Granny was very psychic in her own way. She could read messages and interpret symbols, or get guidance from the hot cinders of the fire. Her readings were so accurate it really was scary. Just before my Granny passed away, she actually did a reading from the hot cinders describing a number of situations prior to her death. Also, she had this gift of attracting feral cats and making friends with them, whereas no one else could get close to them. My Granny was a very special person and in many ways I am like her. Not only in similar build or looks but what I now know is that I too share her psychic abilities. Just like my Granny, I too have a love of cats. For a short period of time I also had a feral cat. Today I have a huge jet-black cat called Sprocket. Sprocket is half Siamese and half Burmese but he too appears to have a psychic tendency! For example, he sits by the telephone just staring at it, and then out of the blue it rings!

4

The Old Portadown Road

This was my parent's first property that they ever bought together. My father left the Royal Navy after serving twenty-five years. Jobs in Lurgan were hard to come by. The only job that was available to Bernard was working in the dye house at the nylon factory. The job itself was not an easy one! It was a dangerous place and working conditions were difficult. My father continued to work at the factory until something more suitable came along. The opportunity did come in the form of what was called in those days the 'GPO'. The letters refer to the 'General Post Office'. My father trained to become a post office telephone engineer. The job meant that he was working outside in all types of weather conditions, erecting telegraph poles and repairing telephone lines, but he was happy and very contented in his new job. Whereas my mother was always happy keeping a nice clean house. She just loved her home and people often complimented her on housekeeping skills. Having four children and with another one on the way, both my parents were kept very busy.

I always remember the family having general traditions connected to that particular house. For example, gathering round early in the evening to say the family rosary. I use to get my brother and sisters into trouble when the rosary was being said, because I would always be performing in some shape, form or fashion and making them laugh. On Sunday afternoons our parents would take the family out and we

11

would walk for miles. Neither of my parents could drive a car; so walking was the only form of transportation around.

That particular house, I often recall from my childhood memories, was always dark, not only in colour but also in atmosphere. Maybe it was due to the fact there was some sort of history attached to that property! Apparently, one of the previous owners, an elderly man, used to live there and had a bit of a reputation. What for? Even today the family are not quite sure. When this man passed away, in those days horse-drawn carriages were used instead of a hearse as now. At the time of the funeral, the horses would not stand still for the undertakers to put the coffin on board the carriage! They had to move the horses further down the road before they could complete their job. Strange but true!

Number 2, the Old Portadown Road unlocked my personal door to a new dimension of having psychic ability! I always felt that our family were not the only ones living there. The hallway, I sensed, was a very *busy* place. I recall sitting in my pram and noticing all these shapes peering at me, but they were strangers. Also, around the top part of the landing area I had always sensed strange vibrations.

My first real encounter with the spirit world came in the form of a past life. I was only three years old, when I had my first encounter, which was that of a past life. My brother, sisters and myself would quite often spend many happy days blackberry-picking with an elderly neighbour called Mrs McGrann. She would make home-made jam, etc. It was returning from one of these berry-picking trips, everyone happily talking, when suddenly I stopped and shouted, 'I have been shot!' 'Don't talk so daft,' was their reply, but I *had* been. After eating some berries, when I shouldn't have, I rubbed my juice-stained hands on my light coloured dress and then it happened. I was no longer a happy three-year-old spending time with loved ones, but a young soldier who was fighting in the trenches and just been shot in the left

12

hand. It was a vision that would not leave me. No one in my family believed me; they thought that I was just an over-imaginative child. Boy, did I prove them wrong! From that day on, strange things started to happen to me and around the house. I started to be aware of things or situations before they had taken place. For example, one day in our enclosed back yard my mother was going to hang out the washing and I was helping her, but the line came away from the wall. My mother, being the practical type, decided to fix the problem herself. I had a vision flash before me, but it was too late: my mother had fallen off the ladder. Luckily she was not hurt, only shocked. In another incident, I knew that I had to stay close to the family pet, a cat called Stripy because I knew she did not want to be alone. Stripy settled down in a box where the firewood was kept in the kitchen and I nestled beside her. Suddenly I called to my parents to come and when they came Stripy had given birth to a very tiny kitten. She only had the one kitten. My parents were amazed about the whole episode. I was left feeling very confused but I could not explain to my family; they would not have understood. The night my younger sister was born, I again had that 'knowing feeling' but could not give any explanation for it. On that particular evening I knew that I had to gather up all my dummies because I sensed someone was coming to live with us and I did not want to share my dummies. Unknown to me I had sensed the birth of a baby, but who would take any notice of me, a mere child!

It was shortly after the birth of Orla that my parents decided to look at other properties. Not only was the family increasing in size but also we started to acquire a number of pets including a donkey called Neddie and Paddy, an Irish terrier. Overall the family feeling of moving out of that house was of great joy. It felt like a huge pressure was lifted off my parents' shoulders. Yet I do have a special happy memory from the Old Portadown Road, that always springs into my present mind, which was my parents walking either side of Neddie the donkey, and me riding him bareback; we were laughing and generally feeling happy.

Even though many years have passed, that house still holds some form of curse over the people who reside there! For example, when the troubles in Northern Ireland were at their worst, someone drove past that house and fired shots into the front room, killing the occupier's son. Since living in that property my mother always insisted that a local priest would bless any future property that we moved to!

5

The Lough Road

The Lough Road was to be our next family home. In Ireland we spell it 'Lough' but in places such as Scotland they spell it slightly differently: 'Loch' Ness. The Lough Road is approximately two miles long and if you continue along it you find the shores of Lough Neagh. This is the largest freshwater lake in the British Isles. Lough Road can only be described as long and straight. The spire of Christ's Church, in Lurgan's Church Place, can be seen in the distance.

The 'corner house' was how my family described our next home. I personally would have described it as a semi-derelict property situated on a corner or bend of the road. It had been empty for many years. I recall that my father acquired the property through a local auction. Although he could not attend the auction, my grandfather went instead and was accompanied by the family solicitor. At the auction the property was showing signs of being very popular among potential bidders. It was at this point that my grandfather instructed the solicitor to bid a hundred pounds over my father's price to secure the sale. My grandfather knew how desperately his son wanted the property and was able to clinch the deal.

The property itself consisted of a hall, living room, kitchen and one main bedroom. There was no bathroom, only a chemical toilet in a tiny outside shed. The house was set in roughly about a quarter of an acre, and it came with its own history. The locals used to call it 'The Haunted House'. To

15

this day I will never know why! Nevertheless, this did not stop my parents from purchasing it. My father always said, 'If a house has four good strong walls you're already halfway there.' It was my father and my brother John who built two new bedrooms from sheets of corrugated iron and timber supports. Those bedrooms are still standing today!

This old house holds a special attachment for me. It was at Lough Road that I was introduced to my first-ever spiritual guide. I remember it so clearly! I was four years old at the time and I recall being woken up from sleep. To my surprise, I found an old man standing by me. He was dressed as a Northern American Indian scout. He spoke to me and said he was known as Indian Joe. I was not frightened but a little bemused because by the left side of the bed there was only a wall. The bed was pushed up so close to the wall, there was no room for anyone to walk by. Indian Joe has been a great comfort to me all through my life-path in general. For example, when I started school at the age of four, I could not wait to go. Previously I would go round the family home and collect all the books with Indian pictures on the front covers and place them in my school bag. I just felt strong inside if I had a picture of Indian Joe with me! My mother was very emotional on leaving me on my first day at school. When we approached the school entrance door, before I could allow my mother to go any further into the school, I said that I was quite okay and could face going on into the classroom on my own! Well, my mother and the headmaster, who was standing close by, were both shocked! The headmaster commented that I was speaking like an adult instead of a four-year-old! At that time I just felt so full of strength because no other child at my school had a North American Indian guide.

The Lough Road always felt like a tiny dolls' house to me but with real people living in it. Everyone was happy and contented residing there. As I mentioned previously,

16

neither of my parents could drive and our house was approximately two miles from Lurgan. My mother would push the pram with my younger sister snuggled up inside. I would sit on what was known as a pram seat. As a child I was always fascinated with certain properties along our usual journey into town but I could not explain why. Buildings in general just seemed to draw me to them and still do today. However, I never felt alone living at that property because when I played in the garden, though my mother could not see me, I always sensed that *someone* was watching me or looking after me. I always felt safe and secure. When our family were sitting together in our living room, I always had a lovely feeling that many other spirit energies shared our family home with us. My psychic ability was slowly developing over a period of time and I did not even realise it. For example, a very old lady called Mrs McNally owned the only shop in our area. She had converted her living room to a small shop, providing essential goods such as bread, fruit, vegetables and milk. All the locals supported the shop, especially the children.

One day my mother asked if Eileen and myself would pop down to the shop to purchase some goods. My brother John decided to accompany us, and brought our Irish terrier Paddy along as well. Mrs McNally was renowned for her love of cats. There were cats everywhere around her property. One cat in particular, a huge grey stripy animal would always sit on the counter! John ordered Paddy to sit and stay outside the shop. Sure enough the big fat cat was lounging in its usual place sunbathing on the counter. Suddenly, I sensed that I had to change the position of where I was standing. It was like a voice telling me to stand in the corner of the shop, but unfortunately I did not move quickly. From nowhere Paddy rushed in and made an attempt to chase the cat. Well the cat did not know what to do and was looking for an escape route. Next moment it jumped up in front of me and bit into my left index finger. My guide was warning me of danger but I was not quick enough to react. Nowadays I read all signs very closely!

Another spiritual incident involved my father not listening to my mother's words of guidance. He decided that the hedge which indicated where the boundary lay needed a good pruning. He told my mother he intended to light a small bonfire but she disagreed and advised him not to. Father, being strong-minded, lit the fire anyway and from nowhere a huge gust of wind came and the hedge actually caught fire. Everyone panicked but luckily no one was hurt and the fire was put out. I believe my mother's psychic gift was forewarning her of the change of weather and the potential danger.

There were more strange experiences for me coming fast and furious. For example, we had lovely neighbours who lived on the opposite side of the road. Their name was Patrick and Mary Dolan. They had a smallholding and bred pigs for a living. They had a huge family, mainly sons, and two daughters. The house I always remembered as being untidy compared to our nice organised home but they had hearts of gold. At that time, as previously mentioned, my little sister Orla became ill. She developed an abscess under her chin, which the doctor thought might be a sign of tuberculosis. It was a trying time for my family because we all had to undergo rigorous tests. Our neighbours the Dolans decided that it would be nice for my mother to come over and watch one of their sows give birth. They thought it would take her mind off her own problems. I went with my mother and I remember watching the birth of these little pink things, practically shooting out one after another from the sow. She had about eight or nine piglets and Patrick reckoned that there was no more to come. Everyone decided it was a long enjoyable evening and my mother was about to take me home. I knew that the mummy pig had something wrong with her and I asked if we could have one last look at the piglets. It was a blessing in disguise because the sow was struggling to give birth to what people call the runt of the litter. I knew Indian Joe was guiding me to get the attention of the adults, so as to help the sow with the last difficult birth! The adults were unaware of what really happened that night.

Another strange incident happened at my local school. I recall the sports day, where the pupils took part in various games. I remember taking part in the egg and spoon race but they needed someone for the three-legged race. When all the events were finished, the children sat down waiting for the results. A little voice told me to prepare myself because my name would be mentioned and I would be the proud owner of a pair of blue rosary beads! Sure enough my team won the three-legged event and I was handed the blue rosary beads. I just accepted the situation because I thought everyone was like me! My parents realised that their children were growing up quickly and needed the comforts of a bathroom, etc. So the search was on for our next property. Overall it was sad leaving Lough Road because everyone had become very attached to that property.

6

172 Shore Road

The Shore Road is best described as the suburban area of Lurgan. The road extends a long way, reaching out to join the countryside. Yet, if you continued you would reach the shores of Lough Neagh, hence the name Shore Road. The family moved there to be near the schools and to my grandparents. However, the property was bought in a hurry because house prices were rising very steeply. This was the only property available and the only downfall was that it had only two bedrooms. My brother John had to use the front sitting room as his bedroom, while the four girls had the front bedroom and my parents slept in the back bedroom. However, it did have a bathroom, which was downstairs. Looking back I would class this property in the same category as the Old Portadown Road because the house always had a very cold feeling.

I can recall my early memories of our family summer holidays. The holiday usually involved long train journeys to Londonderry to visit my Auntie May and her family. Auntie May was my mother's first cousin but it was May's family that had taken my mother in, as previously mentioned. The holiday had always taken place around the July fortnight when all the factories and businesses closed down. My earliest recollection of my auntie's house was when my mother had taken me down for my Uncle Matt's (May's husband) funeral. Auntie May's house was a mid-terrace located in a dead-end street which housed the local branch of British Legion. The house itself had huge bedrooms, really high ceilings and a vestibule door. I always remember certain things about Uncle Matt's funeral. For example, I would have conversations with Uncle Matt and the people around me would contradict me and say, 'But he's passed away darling, he cannot be talking to you.' What they did not know was that I could see and hear him!

After my uncle's passing the house took on a different outlook for me, because I was very confused about the whole situation and no one could give me any answers. While living at 172 Shore Road I became extremely ill and had to be kept in isolation from other family members. The illness was suspected scarlet fever. Luckily I made a full recovery.

During my time at this house, lots of strange things were still happening to me. For example, when the family moved there, Eileen and myself had to change our schools. We got accepted at a school called Tannaghmore, which was just five minutes' walk from our house, whereas Carol, the eldest of the children, went to St Mary's and John went to St Peter's school in Lurgan. Tannaghmore was a Catholic-maintained school. In 1827 the first school in Lurgan was erected on Castor Bay Road. As the population grew the school moved to its present site in 1908. Further extensions took place over the years, as the school became ever more in demand as a result of new housing estates springing up.

It was while I was at Tannaghmore that I felt the urge to suddenly run home. I went with my instinct and when I got home my mother was taken ill with a migraine. She was really ill and needed to be placed in a darkened room. She felt relieved to see me but was cross because I had left school. I was instructed to fetch one of the neighbours who took me back to school and they dealt with my mother.

There were other incidents. For example, I always remember sitting with my father on a Saturday afternoon watching the football results because he used to do the Pools. The Pools coupon involved picking a certain number of football teams and if your teams matched the results on Saturday then you could win money depending on the number of points scored. While watching the results I would say some of the scores before my father heard them on the television. To me it was just a game but my father was mesmerised.

My father sometimes had to go away on courses due to his work. It was on one of these occasions that my mother spotted a lovely house further along Shore Road situated on the corner. Before my father knew anything about it my mother had taken Carol to view the property. Both of them fell in love with it and decided to put in an offer. The offer was accepted straightaway. My mother had to ring my father and tell him what she had done! None of the family was sad about leaving 172 because we had all experienced some sort of strange happening but could not describe them in words!

7

122 Shore Road

What a property! My brother and three sisters thought we had died and gone to heaven when we first saw what was going to be our next family home. 122 Shore Road was a semi-detached house situated on a corner with some wonderful characteristics. For example, the front gardens had huge hydrangeas, which bloomed year after year, and the front door had lovely old-fashioned stained-glass windows, and led into a very spacious hallway. The house also had the widest staircase I have ever seen. Remember I was looking at this property through the eyes of a child. The house used to belong to a well-to-do family who had owned a lot of land, which they sold for residential building. However, the sale of the house was due to a death in the previous owner's family.

Our new house had many grand features such as beautiful fireplaces and a magnificent drawing room, which had a huge bay window plus a smaller window. The whole property was one of great elegance for that particular location. Not that I am a snob but people always looked at our family as if we where well off because we lived in such a beautiful mansion! Many happy times was shared by all the family there.

Carol and John (my older sister and brother) were now young adults and just starting full-time employment. Eileen, my older sister, had now moved up to Saint Mary's secondary school and I was still at Tannaghmore school. Orla was still not old enough to start school. I shared a bedroom with Eileen. It was situated on the corner of the house. This meant we had two windows looking out onto two different roads. We would often complain to our parents about a strange smell in the room. The smell was very pungent, like a mixture of cigar smoke and whiskey. Neither of our parents drank whiskey so how did we know it was that particular drink? My parents changed our bedroom furniture around to see if it would make any difference. Nothing changed. It was obvious that there was an energy of some kind that wanted to get in contact with us. My sister stopped talking about it because she said it was causing trouble for her but I was still pursued by the awful smell.

I recall my early days in that house as being quite happy, playing on my own and making up games and playing houses with my imaginary friends. However, when I went out to play with one particular friend I got into trouble big time! This friend was called Rosemary and she lived only a few doors away from our house. We would take it in turns to play at each other's house but every time I played at Rosemary's house I would see a very old woman in a sitting position all hunched over and wearing dark clothes. I was shocked that no one else could see her and this caused friction between my mother and myself. I would cry and tried to tell everyone that I was not making it up or attention-seeking. In the end my mother told me to stop playing at Rosemary's house. This did not put a stop to the weird things that were happening around me. For example, one day in our kitchen I pointed out to my mother that there were little elf- or pixie-type people dancing around her. 'Don't talk so silly,' was her reply, but were they deliberately trying to get me into trouble? Another incident I recall was my first out-of-body experience, which I had at the age of seven. I remember lying on top of Orla's bed and just looking up at the corner thinking what if I could reach up and touch the corner with my finger?

Wow, I actually did it – by coming out of my body in a floating motion I could touch the corner and return to the bed. Yet I did not see myself as a person when this type of experience happened to me. It was a great new game and I would often tried to sneak away to play the floating game because I just loved the feeling of flying. I decided to keep this new game to myself as it was my secret and I did not want to get into trouble again.

All the rooms in that property held some sort of fascination for me! For example, I would wander into my older sister's bedroom. Carol did not like anyone to touch her make-up but all I was interested in was to talk to the nice lady who had previously lived in our house. The big drawing room was another room where I sensed you were never alone, particularly near the fireplace.

It was at this time that I received my first Communion at Saint Michael's Chapel, because my father's brother was home on leave. He was part of a holy order called the Franciscans but he was based in South Africa. The occasion meant that my poor mother had to go and get all the family new clothes. My first Communion dress had to be bought very quickly and arrangements with the local dressmaker made to have the alterations done promptly. I did feel a sense of being special by having all this fuss made over me and because I would not be sharing my first Communion with all my classmates or anyone else. The chapel was built in 1959, funded by the nuns of the Convent Of Mercy. The nuns made a huge breakfast in my honour. As you probably guessed it, I had great fun talking to the nuns who had previously passed over to the spirit world. I was so fascinated by the whole experience of seeing people that my family could not see. Why me?

I always remember my first introduction to the emotion of anger. I wanted to retrieve my pocket money from a bright red post-box savings container. I asked my mother if she could get my money out for me and she said no because I had to start to respect the value of money. However, temptation was just too strong for me. In the end I became so angry that I went out into the back yard and into the shed. Straight in front of me I saw the axe that my father used for chopping up wood for the fire. Before I knew anything I was like something possessed and I attacked my savings box. On hearing the banging my mother came out, but by that time the poor old savings box was battered to a pulp. In the end I was still not allowed to have my money. However, I realised how anger can really push your emotions to the extent of damaging items that you treasure dearly. I never ever did own another pillar-box red savings box because it would always remind me of the day I lost my temper for the very first time.

There was one other event that happened at the big house that concerned my mother. As children we are really wrapped up in our own world and never stop to notice anything out of the ordinary. For example, one particular evening, although the younger members of the family were usually sent up to bed really early, Eileen was allowed to stay up a bit longer because she was that little bit older. Carol and John were out for the evening, having been given a certain time that they had to be home. I remember waking up that evening with an awful sensation that I was associating a fear connected to my mother. I just felt that my mother was distressed in some way. Then a voice from nowhere was telling me to go back to sleep and all would be well when I woke up. Next day I remember having a feeling that the family would be getting a new addition to the family! However, I had hoped that the new addition would be in the form of a puppy as Paddy and Stripy had long passed to spirit world. I got dressed feeling really excited, and started asking questions. I was told my mother was feeling poorly and was not to be disturbed. No one was allowed near my parents' bedroom and strangers were running in and out of our home. I eventually asked where the puppy was. 'Puppy? What puppy?' my father asked me. I told him the one mummy was getting while I was sleeping. No one could give me a direct answer. My granny was there in our house, which was strange because it was very early in the morning and she never usually visited me that time of day. What was happening was very confusing because I knew something had taken place during the night. I kept insisting I wanted to see the puppy mummy had got. Eventually the penny dropped with my family and they thought it was easier to say that a puppy was brought into the home but died because it was a very poorly puppy. However, what I had originally sensed was that our mother was pregnant and had given birth to a beautiful baby girl, unfortunately stillborn. The event left my family feeling devastated because as kids my mother always wore over-smocks and no one ever commented that another baby was due. Being pregnant in those days was a taboo subject, especially where children were concerned. Our family was allowed to grow up surrounded with pure innocence and, most of all, love. My mother had two further miscarriages following the stillbirth.

As I commented earlier, I was always drawn to certain properties, such as the local grocery shop, which was owned by Jimmy Harrison and his family. This property always held a fascination for me because I could sense people who had passed over still going about their business there as if nothing had happened to them. The shop was dark and gloomy, and always had the smell of decaying vegetation – or was I smelling death? I sometimes felt very sad when I visited that shop.

My parents soon decided that 122 Shore Road held too many painful memories for all of us. After a great deal of thought they decided to move and looked for a property nearer the town, because Carol, John and Eileen were now of an age that they wanted to be out and about with their friends, who all lived in the town centre. Also, my father had the chance of a new job with the GPO, which could be in a different location, so the family would have to be ready to move at a moment's notice. A gentleman called Robert Williams who ran a furniture business but was also like an undercover estate agent found a lovely rented property and suggested that my parents should go and view it very quickly. This property was right in centre of the town, which suited the family's needs. The address of our new family home was 18 North Street!

8

18 North Street

North Street is renowned as one of the longest streets in Lurgan town. It is one of many main streets situated in the town centre. Since the 1901 census North Street has always been portrayed as a self-sufficient street because it had a wide range of shops, a primary school and a Roman Catholic chapel. Today there are even more shops, as residential properties have become commercial premises.

Number 18 will always have a special place in my heart because it was the last home in which all the family were together before they went their separate ways via two marriages and my brother John joining the Royal Navy. The family's first impression of this house was how *old* the building was. Also, the musty smell and the fact that no one had lived in it for a very long time. The house belonged to a Jewish family called Hurst. They had moved to Belfast but kept the family business and residence. The Hurst furniture shop continued to trade in the capable hands of the two young sons. Eli Hurst, the eldest brother, was originally studying to become a dentist. Whereas David, his younger brother, who had a stammer, wanted to become an architect. However, Eli and David had to put their careers on hold because of the sudden death of their father. It was naturally expected that the brothers would carry on the family business. With the help of two female staff, it was business as usual.

When the brothers showed our family around the house we

just could not get over it. We were speechless! The front door was of an imposing size compared to the other neighbours whose doors looked dreary. Also, the furnishings on the door were made of brass. A huge lionshead formed the doorknocker and there was a big round handle. It did not take my mother long to bring the brass furnishings back to their rightful glory. From then on people would often comment to my mother about polishing the door brasses, which she undertook with pride.

The house consisted of a maze of rooms and had a huge, long narrow hallway with ceilings approximately twelve feet high. The front sitting room had a beautiful big archway in the centre of one wall, where there was a beautiful carved cabinet and a really lovely fireplace with a tiny button that you would press for a servant's attendance. A servant was required in this house because of its size. The property dated from around the Victorian period and the Hursts had clearly been well-to-do. There was another room off the hallway but from day one none of the family liked that room because it felt very cold – even with a blazing fire nothing could stop the cold feeling. This room would have been used as a breakfast room but we referred to it as the TV room. Our family gave the room this title because we used it for ironing and watching TV. One remaining door was left and this led you into a lovely long but narrow room with a fireplace that had a huge high mantelpiece. Off this room was the kitchen, which was very tiny, with a white Belfast sink unit and a door leading to the yard and the garden.

The first flight of stairs led onto a small landing with a small but compact bathroom with a suite in the style of Queen Anne, with claw feet on the bath. The door nearest the bathroom led to a lovely cosy bedroom with a very tiny room adjoining it. We thought it might have had two uses. Either a bedroom with a dressing room or a room where the nanny would live and the tiny room a nursery. This was to become my brother John's bedroom.

The second flight of stairs took you to a landing with a further four bedrooms and an additional two flights of stairs leading to the attics. The first bedroom on the left was to become my bedroom that I was to share with Eileen. It had a huge sash window with a view overlooking various next-door neighbours' back yards and outbuildings. You could also see what we called the 'gas house', which was part of the local gasworks whose grounds were next door to our back garden. In addition, there was an orchard that belonged to the National Foresters Club, which was like a social meeting place for men, but women had to be invited as guests.

The front of the house had two even bigger sash windows and a wonderful grey/black marble fireplace. My parents decided this was going to be their bedroom. The third door brought you into a square bedroom that had yet another big sash window, which made the room very bright-looking. Yet it always felt cold, perhaps because it was over the archway that had once allowed horses to come through with deliveries. My younger sister chose this room for her bedroom. The room had another door, which led into a fourth bedroom, and a further door that connected to the furniture shop. Carol decided this bedroom would suit her because being the eldest she wanted some independence and this room was the furthest away for the centre of the house. The room always had a dark, stuffy feel to it and I did not like the connecting door to the shop. This room was also built over the archway. The family used to refer to those particular bedrooms as the 'alley bedrooms'.

Last but not least were the attics. The attic stairs consisted of two flights ascending from the second-floor landing. Climbing the first flight of stairs, which had much narrower steps than the main stairs, brought you to a small landing. This landing had a lovely round porthole-type of window. The view from this window was magical from a child's point of view because one could see beyond the garden boundaries

33

and over the rooftops. The second flight of stairs always had a dark, cold feeling and a disgusting smell – not just musty but something unknown. Inside the attics was a real eye opener because of how bright and spacious they were. The windows were vertex style and the space covered all the area of the house, while the shop had a separate attic. We had to be very careful where we trod because the floorboards were old and some were missing. My parents decided to make the attics an out of bounds area where the children were concerned.

Our family noticed that on all the surrounding door frames there was a little piece of wood about two inches long attached to the frame on an angle. I believe they performed the same function as a holy water font just inside a door, in which one would dip one's fingers to bless oneself. The Jewish people would rub this tiny piece of wood in the same way. My parents use to give the tiny icons a rub before they went to bingo to increase their luck, and sometimes it worked!

Attached to the property was a very spacious oblong back yard that could easily accommodate two vehicles parked side by side. The yard was surrounded by various outbuildings all shapes and sizes. Most of the outbuildings were used for storage purposes for the Hurst family. One was used as a garage. Inside it was Mr Hurst senior's car, which the family could not bear to part with when their father died. The car was in immaculate condition and would have been described as a classic car of its time. Often the brothers would drive the car out into the yard to wash it or just to make sure the engine was still in working order. Beside the garage there was an area that had a huge pile of small rocks. Even to this day no one really knows what this was for. Towards the back of the long yard was a wall-enclosed garden with a large privet hedge mixed with ivy to form an archway over the garden gate. My father decided that the hedge was going to be his first project but my mother had other jobs for him such as painting and decorating. This garden can only be

34

described as a secret garden because it looked so sad and neglected when we moved into the property. Little did our family know the strange effect the garden was going to have on various members, such as feeling melancholy, and none of us could really play for long periods in the garden. I shall reveal more information on that later in the book.

Moving away from the garden, the sheds on the left-hand side of the yard were absolutely full of old cardboard boxes etc. One of the sheds was to become our coal shed, as the family nicknamed it. Our back door was close to this shed and there was also an entrance to the small yard that could be seen from my bedroom window. The small yard was to become home to our new family pet, a Golden Labrador called Sandy.

That poor house was very neglected and just crying out for someone to love it. Enter the Ferris family; and boy, did we bring it back to being a proper home again!

North Street suited all the family requirements. My mother made number 18 a home to be proud of. All the front windows were dressed in the same curtain material and fresh flowers were always on show in the sitting-room window. The front door was repainted, plus the outside of the house, and all the door brasses shone brightly.

I really grew attached to that house in a strange kind of way. On the other hand, odd events would take place around our new home but especially in the room we called our living room. Items would simply fall off the dining table but no one would be near them, and we would laugh and joke about it. Or the door would open and the curtains would move without any assistance of a physical nature. I recall my mother sitting in that room and getting up out of her chair because she had seen a reflection of a man go by. When she checked the back yard no one was there.

The front sitting room my mother classed as the 'good room' and was only used on special occasions such as

Christmas or other social events. The sitting room was warm and welcoming and had a very serene feeling. Indeed, it was in that room that I started to self-develop my gift without even realising it. I would stand in the centre of the window and close my eyes. Inwardly, I would be asking for help from my guardian angels and those who had passed over to send my friends who were calling at our house to go roller-skating to hurry up. Also, in my mind's eye I would say if a red car passed by, then my friends would knock at the front door, and sure enough a red car would go by and my friends would be knocking at the door! My friends would say, 'Were you standing by the front door?' because the door would open immediately.

Looking back, my mother would always go into the front sitting room after Sunday lunch for what was known as forty winks! This became a regular occurrence but in a way my mother was relaxing or meditating because she would always feel fresh and clear-thinking after these sessions. I always used the room to practise difficult steps when I was involved with Irish dancing. Because of the room's calming effect I felt like I had my own personal teacher telling me the format of the dance routine. It's strange because when I entered my first *feis* (the Irish name for a dancing competition), I stood out because my mother could not afford to buy me a dancing costume, which cost a lot in those days. Instead I wore my first Communion dress and I had this strange feeling that I would give a good performance and be in the top three. Where that thought came from I do not know. I had not been long taking dance lessons so it was a bit of a shock for the family that I was asked to take part. Lo and behold I was given third place and received a medal. However, it did not go down very well with those pupils who had been going to dance class longer than me.

My younger sister Orla never liked the bedroom that I shared with our older sister Eileen. I recall one particular event – Orla came racing down the stairs. She claimed that she had seen the lady dressed in blue who was the mother of Jesus, meaning the Blessed Virgin. To this day no one can talk her out of what had taken place in that bedroom.

As children we tended to play in the house because we had plenty of rooms to play games such as hide and seek etc. Nevertheless, as kids each of us was drawn towards the attics. In a way, we where frightened because we knew that the attics were unsafe but it was a mixture of a creepy but exciting feeling at the same time. Playing on the first flight of stairs you would feel a warm comforting sensation. However, when you moved from the small landing that divided the two flights of stairs it was cold and you could see your own breath even though my father had blocked off the draughts that were coming from the attics. It was not the cold feeling that unnerved me but the voices of whispering children. When I asked my family if they had heard the voices they just looked at me with blank expressions. I can recall a past memory of mine when I was about ten years old. I would sit at the top of the first flight of stairs, which was painted a dark brown colour, and chalk up how many days were left to Christmas. My parents didn't tell me off for doing this but it felt like someone who lived there before me had done the exact same thing.

I loved my parents' bedroom, not only because it was a huge room but also I used to stand and look out of the right-hand window. It was like a magnet drawing me to come and look out, or was I just reliving another past memory of a female who had lived here before, waiting and watching for her loved one to return home? Yet, the window on the left-hand side never had the same appeal. The view from my favourite window allowed me to see the town clock, which was built into the local church spire, just peeking above the other buildings. I sensed that I was not the only person who had checked the time from this viewpoint. My mother would often be found gazing out of the same window in the same direction as I did and the past energies before us.

Also, when I stood at this particular window and looked directly at the houses opposite I would see people dressed in what only could be described as old-fashioned clothing from the Victorian period. Their furniture was of the same era and there was no electricity but only candles lighting up the rooms. When I questioned my family about this I was a told off and banned from looking out of my favourite window. This type of telling off made me feel very confused at times because my family would say I watched too much television or had too vivid an imagination.

As mentioned, our back garden had a very creepy feeling about it. My father would only spend about an hour or two at a time in the garden, which was not like him because he generally loved the outdoor life. The garden was divided into two by a long straight pathway that led to a derelict base where a greenhouse or summerhouse had once stood. Close by was a very old pear tree, which kept on trying to bear its fruit, but it was ancient and the fruit just tasted woody. Also, there were a few small apple trees but again they never really gave us any fruit. On entering the garden to the left was what would have been a beautiful Victorian garden but sadly it had neglected flowerbeds, surrounded by tiny wall edgings in an array of shapes such as circles. My father tried to make this a pretty garden for my mother but nothing would ever grow there; it was as if part of it had died with a previous life. Dad would just say the soil was old and very poor rather than admit that an outside energy had a hold over the garden. The vegetable plot on the opposite side of the garden fared better. My father had brought it back to life by growing potatoes, carrots, radishes, etc. Even the old gooseberry bushes provided the Ferris family with extra fruit.

When I went into the garden I would have the same sensation as in the attics: that someone was watching me, and I was never alone in the garden. Maybe it was the voices of children from the past, who once frequented the garden as I did, calling me.

My mother first had her clothes line put up in that garden but then she made my father put it in the main yard area. I never really knew why she insisted on the change of position, but I can guess.

The year 1966 will always remain in my mind. Not only was it the year that England beat West Germany in the World Cup final but it was at that time that I cut my left hand. The incident happened when I fancied a crusty bread roll and I required an adult to cut the roll for me because as children our mother was very protective of use of sharp items such as knives. I asked my parents if one of them could cut open the roll but I was told to wait because England were about to score a goal. However, I became very impatient and took on the responsibility of cutting the bread roll. The knife slipped and cut me badly between my left thumb and index finger. In fact, this was the same hand I recalled being shot in my past life as a young soldier. My father practically ran me all the way down to our family doctors where I had my hand stitched up, but the strange thing is I had always wanted to see into my doctor's home – little did I think it would be under those circumstances.

My over-active imagination was always causing me to get into trouble and I felt it was not right to bring strangers into my world of communicating with others who had passed over to the spirit world, so it was still my secret. I would often play with two sisters called Anna and Brigid Lynch. The Lynch family only lived a street away from our house. When I played at their house I would always ask questions about the families who had lived there before the Lynch family moved in. The Lynch sisters thought it even more peculiar when I questioned them about the array of photographs that was displayed in their front room. The photos on the piano always drew my attention especially any family group shots because I could never see their father in the photographs, but they said he was in the picture. Once again, it would appear that I was causing some kind of strange confusion and my mother thought it was better if I played within 'our four walls' as she used to put it. However, it was not long after the incident concerning the missing Mr Lynch that our family heard he died very suddenly and there was no illness or anything else that could have detected an early death.

The question I was thinking at that precise time in my life was, why was I so different from my family and friends? I would keep asking myself this same question over and over again in my mind. All through my childhood and into adulthood, I always felt that both my parents but especially my mother were always very protective towards me. It was almost as if someone from a higher plane had given them orders to take care of me.

I can recall how I should have been listening to my mother's warning of 'always be aware of the busy traffic' before crossing the road. We were about to set off on the family summer holiday, a week's stay in a caravan in Newcastle, County Down. My mother decided to send me up to our local fish and chip shop, which was owned by Italians. I was really excited about going on holiday and I nearly forgot my mother's usual warning, were it was not for the fact that I felt someone or something accompanying me to the chip shop. On my return journey the pre-holiday nerves got the better of me and I nearly stepped out in front of a car; but something pulled me back onto the pavement. Personally, I believe it was the work of my guardian angels looking after me because for one quick moment I allowed my logical mind to be distracted by another thought.

The house move meant that us children had to change primary schools. This was hard for me because I was so used to having boys in my class and being taught by a male teacher, whereas my new school was called the Sacred Heart and my new teachers where mainly nuns from the local convent, the Sisters of Mercy. Other female teachers taught at this establishment too. The school itself was positioned on Market Street, the heart of the town centre. The building itself was very old and dark, and had that smell which was always associated with schools. It was the only school where I hated being nominated to take the register back to the headmistress's office because you felt that you where being followed by the spirits of the past. Or was it the stories of the nun's head in the bottle that may have put the fear of God into me? Again I allowed myself to stop thinking rationally because what I can sense was the energies of past pupils wanting to be my friend, but instead I listened to the strange tales. How confusing was my short-lived period at that school, because it was almost like someone or something was watching over me and eventually answered my prayers to get out of that school. My prayers were answered because a mistake was made in my transfer from my previous school to the current one. This meant I would skip a year at the primary school and go straight into the secondary school, called Saint Mary's Intermediate School. There were two entrances, Arthur Street and Warring Street; I used the nearest one which was Warring Street. This street could only be described as a derelict row of houses except for a few, because the local council had future plans to rebuild the street with modern homes. Again I would sense a feeling of energies still occupying these empty houses that were once part of a thriving community. Not only could I hear but I would also see them going about their business as if they still lived on the earth plane.

Saint Mary's also had one or two cold spots within the building and outside as well, as I started to recognise the familiar signs such as feeling cold or getting warm when everyone else was feeling the normal room temperature.

41

Speaking of temperatures, what a strange experience I had when I first started at this school. All through my childhood I was forever plagued with tonsillitis because I had huge enlarged tonsils. As a result, my tonsillitis played up and I was sent packing to hospital but I was not alone because our family doctor was of a practical nature and sent Orla in as well to have the same operation. However, Lurgan Hospital had a different use in Victorian times – it used to be a poor house. My mother used to work at the hospital and often mentioned strange goings on such as paperwork going missing from the offices and strange sightings of staff with peculiar uniforms. When in hospital I experienced a similar thing. Just after my operation I recall waking up feeling thirsty. I thought it was night-time because the room gave me the feeling of darkness and I remember calling out for a drink of water. Next thing from nowhere stood by my bed was a person who wore a strange uniform and she assisted me with the offer of water. However, I noticed she never acknowledged me when I said thank you as our parents always taught the family to be polite at all times. As a result of my night drink I was feeling sick and had to call out for help again. When the nurse came I noticed she was wearing the more modern uniform and she commented about a water jug by my table because I was nil by mouth I was not allowed anything until the consultant had been round. I told her about the nurse in the older uniform and she confirmed a nice person who no longer worked there but kept popping in had visited me. It did not stop there because I used to play with a lovely little blonde-haired girl. I noticed how all the other everyday sounds would no longer be heard, her voice was all I could hear. I was sad when she left to go home and I got my mother to ask her whereabouts; but no one had seen or heard of the little blonde-haired girl. Was she just one of the many spirit energies that I was now becoming aware of?

Like I said, Saint Mary's had some places that gave you

the creeps, such as around the stage and the assembly hall, which always felt a bit uncomfortable to me. There were whispering voices but I could not pinpoint where they came from. Everywhere I went they seemed to follow me so I just tried to blank them out as I thought that was how my friends dealt with the situation. Little did I know that I was the only one who was in tune with spirit world. Even our headmistress would answer phone calls when no one was on the receiving end and doors would open and close all by themselves and the fire bell would go off for no reason. I often wondered why the school had so many different caretakers. Was it something that had taken place within the school or what? Unknown to me again, I would be nurturing my gift without realising it because when I entered competitions such as an essay or talent competition I always knew that I would win a prize.

I used to have this feeling of wanting to return to the family home at North Street, because I always felt very secure there and I cannot really find the reason why. Each of my family members always had this type of secure feeling about the property.

As my brother and sisters were becoming more independent and enjoying a full working and social life I began to notice how they would approach my mother and ask her to do their cards for them. This intrigued me because my father did not like my mother dealing with playing cards and she would use them when he was not around. Whether he associated it with gambling, I was not sure. I was the only one who really showed an interest in what my mother could do with just normal playing cards. I would sit very quietly and watch closely how she dealt the cards and the funny way she would join them all to form a wedding bed. If this formation broke in the process of turning it over it was a sign of a broken engagement or marriage. I was fascinated by the whole business of dealing the cards and reading messages that could change life's direction. However, I never once heard my mother relay messages from people who had passed over to the spirit world.

If there was a wake, as we call them in Ireland, when a person's remains are brought back to their family's home for a period of rest for twenty-four hours, people would come to the home and say their last farewell and pay respects to the family. People would indulge in a party atmosphere, eating, drinking and recollecting stories from the past. It is said that the corpse should never be left alone for that period. I was not bothered about such things, even when you had to kiss the body as a sign of respect. In general I always felt honoured because I never viewed the corpse as being dead but as someone who has started their journey to a better place.

I knew that a time would come when the family would go off in their own directions. The first family sibling to leave home was my older brother John, who was joining the Royal Navy and following in my father's footsteps. Next was Carol, who left the family home to get married. Next was Eileen, whom I shared a bedroom with. She left not only to get married but also to live in England. Our house seemed to be even bigger now that the family had shrunk down to four, including my parents.

Life as a young teenager was not that of a normal thirteen-year-old because I had decided to try and find how and why these things were happening only to me. At school I would ask my friends if they ever had seen anything unusual, or did anything out of the ordinary ever happen to them? The answer was always the same: NO.

The strange happenings were now becoming more regular. One day while I was at Saint Mary's I was getting some books from a cupboard when I had a vision that Miss O'Neil, a teacher, was going to enter the classroom. In fact, I just got closing the cupboard door when the said teacher entered the classroom. How bizarre was that? At home I tried to tell

44

my parents what was happening around me and at one point my mother asked one of my older sisters to find out if I was taking drugs of some sort.

I will never forget the day that my father was involved in a freak type of accident. Orla and myself were at school when my mother received the terrible news about my father's accident. Apparently, he had climbed up a thirty-foot high telegraph pole and strapped himself in the safety harness when the pole broke four feet from the ground. My father's main fear was landing on the railway track which lay close to the area where he was working. The result was that he could no longer continue to do his job because he had trapped some nerves and lost the power of his hand. Therefore, an office job was set aside for him when he eventually returned to work. The accident changed everyone's life, most of all my parents. They decided that North Street was far too big with only two young daughters left at home and so another home must be found. About a year later my father's sister and her family had just moved to a new housing estate called Drumbeg South in Craigavon. My auntie spoke of how quickly the houses were being allocated and so my parents must act fast if they wanted one. An application form was sent to the local council offices and as luck was on the side of the Ferris family we got allocated a new house. My parents broke the news to the Hurst brothers who were as devastated as we were about the move. It was a very sad time for the Ferris family leaving North Street because we had some wonderful neighbours and had made loads of friends.

Overall my emotions told me that no other property would come up to the standard of North Street because of its unique spiritual and loving atmosphere.

However, after we left another family moved in to rent the property and only stayed there two weeks because some family members had to be put on medication due to poltergeist activities within the house.

9

Drumbeg South

Drumbeg South was a small estate of residential houses that belonged to the huge new town Craigavon. The town was built between two major towns, Lurgan and Portadown. New developments such as this one were intended to take the overspill of families from Belfast. However, the project proved to be at fault because people did moonlight flits, such as moving without telling anyone where they were going or not paying any of their outstanding bills. Therefore, vandals saw the perfect opportunity to move in and wreck large amounts of the surrounding properties. Also, this was a time when Northern Ireland was in the height of a religious dilemma. In fact, this had contributed to the housing situation because Catholics and Protestants did not want to live side by side. Drumbeg South was not a pretty estate by any means because the houses just looked like rows of concrete rabbit hutches. They all looked the same except for the different coloured curtains or blinds that dressed repetitive windows on the dreary terraces.

Our new home was positioned at the end of a terrace on the edge of the estate and we had a main road just the other side of the fence boundary. We shared a strip of footpath with a line of eight other houses. There was a car park at the opposite end of the terrace.

I was about sixteen years old when my family decided to moved to Drumbeg South. The new family home made us feel like we where living in a goldfish bowl because it was open plan downstairs, and upstairs we had two average-sized bedrooms plus a box room that was classed as a third bedroom. Not forgetting the family bathroom, which was small. The open plan lounge/dining room had windows reaching from floor to ceiling and stretched the length of the house with a glass door that opened onto the back garden. Our front door was also made of clear glass so my mother immediately put up a heavy curtain to have some sort of privacy from the peering eyes. We had blown-air central heating which was novel because it was one main hollow shaft placed in the centre part of the house and if you were in the bathroom you could hear the television and family conversations. This house was a strange home because my mother always kept beautiful homes wherever she lived. However, in this house she could not make the furniture fit. Consequently, there was the uncomfortable feeling of not being wanted. My father could not bring himself to do anything with the back garden, which was open plan with only two strips of wire separating us from the neighbours. My parents never really unpacked so most of our personal belongings were still in boxes in the loft or stacked up in the built-in wardrobes. Everyone in the family was feeling very heavy hearted and so we tried to cheer each other up by talking about making a new life and all that entails.

Not long after we moved in I got a new job working in a sewing factory that produced items made from Irish linen that would eventually end up being sold abroad. Gradually my sister and I started to make new friendships from all age groups. Our cousin lived close by so she helped us to settle down in an alien environment.

Well, that is how my family felt regarding the house move. We sensed that this change would only be a temporary measure and we only stayed there for about two years. I eventually settled down into a routine and began to chum around with two girls, Frances and Anna, who were the same age as me.

48

Actually Frances and I worked together in the same factory. It was at that house that I had a sleepwalking experience for the last time. It felt like I had come into the life of a person who suddenly woke up and realised they were late for work. It was a good thing that my mother intervened and stopped me before I dashed out the front door only half dressed. The weird thing was that it felt such a natural routine still under the influence of slumber.

My first experience of being curious about paranormal activities was when a group of friends decided they would like to investigate an empty property just four doors down from where I lived. Strange but true, I would always hurry past this house even when it was occupied by a family who had a young toddler. Rumour had it that the young family had to leave due to the fact that the property required fumigating or was this a fib to stop people from entering the house? A disturbing fact about the design of the front doors to these properties was that one could illegally unlock the door. By putting your hand through the letterbox, with the aid of a stick you could manoeuvre the lock till the door opened. This was why many of the properties had squatters residing in them. Once the group had entered the property I knew it was a bad idea because straight away I saw dark shadows and a misty effect in the room. As the group sat on the cold damp floor in a circle I looked around and it was very dark and creepy with only a little ray of light coming from a nearby street lamp. Everybody had to sit quiet and not make a noise. Kevin, the leader of the group because he was the eldest, asked in a reasonable tone if there were any spiritual beings with us and if so would they present themselves. As of that moment I began to feel very cold even to the point of shivering uncontrollably because it felt like someone or something was whispering in my ear and I could stand it no longer, so I screamed. In fact, at that point the entire group was falling over each other trying to escape from the house and whatever else was emotionally involved with the property. The noise brought the surrounding neighbours out including my parents and they were not very happy with me. So for the next few days I stayed in rather than go upsetting anyone, plus I needed time on my own to get over what I had just experienced. The group wanted to know what happened in that house and I just replied that I felt overcome with fear. They went along with my story. Another ghost-hunting event was arranged for a Sunday afternoon; no one would be suspicious of a group of teenagers going out for a country walk. The location was a derelict farmhouse situated in fields close to the new housing estate. I recall it being a bright summer afternoon when we met up and headed off across the fields towards the haunted property. I kept back my true feelings of what I really was sensing about this haunting issue because the members of the group would not understand that I had the gift of connecting to situations before they happen. When we arrived at the property Kevin decided to split us up into three groups to make it easier to explore the area. Well, my group was full of excitement whereas I sensed an unknown fear, or was it because I knew we were being watched by the family who had lived there numerous years ago? I suddenly started to call out names but these names belonged to the different individuals who no longer lived on the earth plane. How did I have knowledge of this personal information? Next instant, the entire group came dashing out of the building and I must admit I ran too because a little girl called Jenny was tugging my clothes and asking me to be her friend. At that point I felt my own fear and shivers run down my back and that was when I screamed and ran for it. Jenny, the spirit child, shouted to me that the house was not burning any more. None of my friends from the group would ever talk to me about what happened on that particular day, and I sometimes wonder why. Indeed, that was the last time the group decided to go ghost-hunting.

Not long after that incident there was another strange occurrence when I was at home alone. A gypsy was doing the rounds of the houses selling lucky heather. I recall my mother always saying, 'If a gypsy asks for a cup of water you give it to them plus let them keep the cup.' So when the old gypsy knocked on the door she did not ask for a cup of water but wanted money to tell my fortune. Feeling shocked I refused because I only had fifty pence left to my name. I offered this to the woman but she refused. I immediately thought, my God I have offended a gypsy, I will be cursed for life, but no. She did say some strange things to me, such as, you will be corresponding from across the sea and you will marry and have two children. This strange old woman looked as if she knew everything about the past, present and the future. I was only seventeen and this was my first ever experience of fortune telling, which baffled me. Was she right or wrong?

My friend Frances had informed me of a new youth club and maybe it might be fun and a chance to meet the local talent (guys). So we decided to give it a go. We noticed that there were plenty of lads around of similar age to us. I had a weird and wonderful feeling that I would be talking to a blond-haired lad before the end of the evening. Call it a premonition. A really good looking blond-haired lad called Connor sat next to me and asked me to go out with him. Well, this simply blew my mind. Was it fate or was it spirit energy drawing two people closer together? It was hard for me to understand what was happening to me because I would sense something and it would actually happen. Nevertheless, I had to get used to it and consequently it just kept repeating throughout my life path. My personal experience of life was starting to include how sensitive I was becoming towards the negative aspects of people's emotions. Also, my psychic interest in buildings was growing more intense. Gradually, I was changing and my friends began to notice that I was a little bit different to them because I was tuning in to the spirit world. Therefore, my friends thought I was being rude by ignoring them or not joining in their conversations or activities. In actual fact, sometimes I would describe a scenario to them and after a short space of time it would happen. For example, every Saturday evening we would go for a walk which included passing the local shopping centre with its residential pub to see if there was anyone we knew around. I call to mind on one occasion during our walk I had a hunch that we would bump into an army patrol or road block. As we turned a corner there was an army patrol just setting up a road block. There were soldiers dashing around with their faces all blackened and jeeps angled so cars would have to stop for random searches. As we hurried past in fear of snipers my mind was working overtime wondering, where did that powerful information come from? After that occasion I was determined to explore further, with amazing results such as guessing what colour clothes my friends would be wearing or who would be telephoning before I answered. My eighteenth birthday was coming up so my parents said I could have some friends around to celebrate. By this time I had met Danny, a trainee draftsman from Londonderry. We started going out together which pleased both sets of parents. On the evening of my party I had invited two brothers who I got to know really well, but they lived in Lurgan which was about ten minutes' drive away. Tommy, the elder of the two brothers, had his own delivery business. He was the life and soul of any party but I just sensed a sadness about him. I could not quite put my finger on why. Two days after my party it was announced on the local news that Tommy had been shot in his family home; another sectarian murder. I was feeling unwell and asked myself if I could have warned him of the danger that lay ahead of him. Would he have listened or thought I was just barking mad? When my parents said they had found a new home, a bungalow, my younger sister and I were ecstatic. The days were being counted until we could move out and leave the goldfish bowl for good.

10

Ardowen

Ardowen is situated in the new Craigavon development on the outskirts of the expanding township. This new estate had a combination of two and three bedroom properties plus six bungalows. The houses were a concrete construction but the builders had applied a lighter colour. However, the format of terracing was very much the same. This new estate had local amenities such as a grocery shop and a Roman Catholic church called Saint Anthony's. The day came when my parents collected the new keys from the Housing Association. My mother was excited as we approached the entrance of the cul-de-sac where our new house was. Our new home was located third on the left-hand side with garages in a semi-circle to give each of the houses more privacy. The moment we entered the new dwelling I immediately had mixed emotions. Why did I not identify the sensation? What was I picking up on? No one had ever lived there before; it was a newly-built house on farmland. As we entered the hallway, to the left was an average size kitchen which had a door into a long-shape lounge/dining room. Just off from the lounge/dining room were a further two doors. One led into a small bedroom which my younger sister Orla had. I did not like that room for some reason; it was kind of creepy. Starting from the lounge/dining room there was a huge window and glass door that took you out to the garden. Another door from this room took you back into the hallway. The hallway itself was of a good size with a glass door directly opposite the front door that opened onto the square back garden area. Off the main hallway was a long narrow corridor leading to my parents' bedroom which was always bright and sunny even in winter. My bedroom was a long-shaped room and the atmosphere was always cold. Yet, when I had it decorated in a lovely lilac colour, which in later years I was informed was a very spiritual colour, weird things happened; I sensed there was others in this room with me. Finally, the last of the three doors led to a very tiny room which became a room for my sister and me to entertain our friends. We had a separate toilet and bathroom area which was great because as two young teenagers we used to spend hours in the bathroom getting ready. Overall the bungalow always felt negative as the rooms had a gloomy type of feeling associated with them and no matter what you did to change the atmosphere it stayed the same.

A new leisure centre was built near our home in Ardowen and this opened up a variety of job opportunities. My mother applied with her friend Joan to be morning cleaners and they both got taken on. However, they were still short of catering staff so I sent in an application form, went for an interview and got the job, which involved shift work but I did not mind. This new job suited me because my home was only ten minutes away. The moment I started my new job I felt that I could hear voices but not associated with those that worked alongside me. Nearly all the time the door would open into the kitchen but no one would be there or kitchen appliances would just switch off. There were no explanations as to why things like this should take place. Strange unexplained things started happening around the leisure centre. Some of the staff even started to attribute the happenings to an invisible person called Harry but I sensed there was more than just Harry being mischievous. It was not long before my mind was full of other important things like Danny, who was my first full-time relationship. Danny and I had been seeing each other over a long period so it was obvious that one day we would become engaged and this actually happened. Danny introduced me to a married couple who were a lot older than us. From the moment I met this couple it just never felt right because Danny and Pete would always be in a huddle whispering so that Karen and myself could not overhear their conversations. Actually this was the start of me beginning to ignore the signs from my spirit guides because I should have been a little bit more observant. Unknown to me Danny was involved with a paramilitary organisation as a junior leader. Pete was his commanding officer but they portrayed the situation as good friends who wanted to take their partners out for meals and drinks; what a perfect cover for their sham. One dark winter's night about 10.45 p.m. my family was getting ready to retire for the evening when there was a loud knocking at the front door. My mother opened it only to find Pete standing in a parka jacket. His hood was up and you would hardly recognise him as this funny bloke who was renowned for telling jokes. He spoke only in a gruff voice asking or telling my mother that he needed to speak to me. When I approached the door I felt a rush of fear rise within me. This was not a good feeling, my intuition was telling me over and over again. I painfully listened to the harsh message Pete was giving me. He explained that he and Danny were on so-called manoeuvres and there was a breakdown in communications and this put their task into jeopardy. As a result, Danny got caught but Pete had escaped and was now a wanted man. As he spoke I was listening to other voices from nowhere telling me it would never work with Danny and his paramilitary connections because we would never have a future together. Not long after that eventful evening I visited the Long Kesh prison just after some of the inmates attempted to burn it down but they only damaged some detention centres. As the prison bus was taking the visitors to the visiting block the vision I witnessed was a phoenix rising from the ashes of the burnt down encampment. This time I did acknowledge this particular sign and I knew I had to break off the engagement based on the previous information that the voices had given to me. In fact, my spirit guides showed me a mental image of Danny being long-term in prison and this was not part of my future life path. I tried to explain to family and friends but again it was the same old story; I got deeper into trouble trying to put into plain words that my future did not include Danny. After Danny I started going over to the nearby township of Portadown because there was a disco twice a week and most of my friends had started going over in a taxi there and back. My parents were not very happy about me going because the troubles seemed to be getting worse and not better. I had only been going over to Portadown for about four weeks when different people approached me and told me that someone called Joe O'Hara wanted to ask me out but was too shy to do so. I eventually gave in and we started dating on a regular basis. As a result I ignored a number of important signs telling me not to go out with Joe. Joe and I got engaged and about eighteen months later we where planning our wedding. However, unknown to me my family was not keen on the idea of the marriage and when the fateful day arrived there were a lot of signs so obviously suggesting this marriage would never succeed. For example, Carol was ironing the wedding dress and she accidentally scorched it, plus the priest had double-booked the wedding service and had to dash between the two chapels. Furthermore, as the wedding car was approaching the big church in the town centre a lonely sniper shot rang out, the target being a policeman on duty outside the local police station. Why did I let my emotions get the better of me? Surely a lay person would connect the signs as to how the future would lie between Joe and me? My new matrimonial home was already chosen by Joe's family. The O'Hara family lived in a small housing estate which consisted of houses, maisonettes and old-age pensioners' flats. Apparently, one of the maisonettes was about to come up for rent due to the death of the current owner. As a result, Joe's family took it upon themselves to secure it for us. However, they did this without consulting me. After a doomed honeymoon, married life was to begin at the ill-fated Parkside Portadown.

11

22 Parkside

22 Parkside was situated in an area of Portadown locally named the Tunnel because you had to travel under the railway bridge which was part of the highway leading to the town centre. In the height of the troubles in Northern Ireland the Tunnel was renowned as one of the main flashpoints. Joe and his family had taken possession of the keys of our new home. Plus they had shown all and sundry around the maisonette before I had chance to see it. This had taken place about four weeks before we got married. The split second Joe turned the door key I knew it was a big mistake. I sensed a chilly shiver pass through my spine even though it was a baking hot day in late June. This property did not have a pleasant feeling because it was almost as if someone invisible to the naked eye was hissing and pushing you from the moment you entered. As you entered the maisonette you were faced with a flight of stairs that brought you to a small landing with two doors and another flight of stairs. The first door led to the open plan lounge and dining room plus another door bringing you to a tiny kitchen with an antiquated drying cupboard which I hated. The second door on the landing was a large storage cupboard. The second flight of stairs took you to another landing which had three doors. First was a large front bedroom that felt very cold and lifeless. The second bedroom was stifling and I felt as though I would pass out if I did not get out. The bathroom was tiny and again did

not have a nice feeling. Later I found out to my cost what was behind the horrible energy; it was to do with the previous tenant. Rumour had it that the old man was of a rather large size and would never leave his home so instead young boys would run daily errands for him until something happened and none of the boys would go near the maisonette again. Joe and I moved in just after our honeymoon. Life continued as routine for Joe except he would enter his new home and not his family residence. Joe was an apprentice baker with under a year to do before he would be fully qualified. As for myself, I had to give up my previous job and take up new employment at a nearby sewing factory producing women's lingerie. I hated and detested every moment of it because the factory had bad vibes and negative feelings. Also, I must have been tuning into everyone's emotion perception because I would feel totally drained when I got home. The maisonette was our first and last matrimonial home. Furthermore, there was a sign of previous unconstructive force that was still associated with the property which made my life pure torment because I became a victim of both mental and physical abuse from my newly-wedded husband. First signs of trouble came when Joe's family started dictating how we should live, eat and organise our lives. Joe did nothing about the situation so I had to grin and bear it hoping for a transformation to happen. Before Joe and I got married we were happy in our own way. Yet my family saw a change in my behaviour, saying I was short-tempered towards them and this would only happen when I spent a weekend at Joe's family home. Joe and I had just taken possession of a second-hand black and white television set and we were so looking forward to watching a new programme called *Charlie's Angels*. In fact, it was a bit uncanny, that title, because later in my life-path I was introduced to my angels and since then I have worked very closely with them. Just as the TV show started, from simply nowhere Joe, who was sitting by me on the settee, lunged at me and started beating me for no apparent reason. This was an unprovoked attack and I immediately became his victim. Following the assault he sat down and cleared his throat and said he was under a lot of pressure at work. What he was not telling me was that he had got a final warning at work because his efforts were not up to standard. I went to bed that night petrified he was going to attack me again. Another disturbing incident happened a few weeks later while I was sleeping alone because Joe had to get up at 3.00 a.m. to be at work by 4.00. I was barely getting that nice tired feeling again when suddenly I sensed movement on the bed. It felt as if someone or thing had put its weight on the bottom of the bed and was moving towards me. In my mind I was calling out to all and sundry to protect me from what I was about to face. At that precise moment I stretched out and switched on the bedside lamp only to find evidence that something unknown of a heavy weight had left a huge indent on the mattress. Also I was aware that I was the only one in the maisonette and what had taken place was it an illusion; or had the spirit of our predecessor decided to make his presence known? I slept with the light on after that. A number of unexplained incidents happened around our home. When I was cleaning around the landing area it felt like I was being shoved or pushed down the stairs. Items would be changed around, especially anything to do with my family. For example, my parents bought the both of us a beautiful dining room set as our wedding present. I came home from work and noticed how my family photographs and ornaments had been moved but this time there were big visible scratches all across the top of the dining-room cupboard. I asked Joe if he had done it but these things was happening when we where out. Numerous unexplainable things were happening in the region of our dwelling. When I enquired with Joe's family about the strange comings and goings I was told that there was nothing going on within our home and I just had a very vivid imagination. Therefore, for my own interest it was best not to disclose to any of the neighbours about these events. Neighbours? What are they? No one had spoken to me or acknowledged me since the day I moved in. The troubles in Northern Ireland were getting worse and there was much unrest around the Tunnel district of Portadown. One night Joe and I had just got into bed when I heard a whizzing noise coming past the window from outside. Joe proudly informed me that was the sound of a sniper's bullet searching for its target. Once more fear of a different type swept over me. What type of place had Joe brought me to? The situation between Joe and me got worse because he would lash out at me for no reason. I was like a permanent petrified rabbit, frightened all the time. Joe could be described as a Jekyll and Hyde character because he had a split personality. One minute he could be nice as pie and the next he could kill you if he wanted to. Also, he had a obsession with fire and one night while waiting for the bus home to Portadown I had an uneasy feeling and the next moment Joe's jacket was on fire where he had been striking the lighter inside his jacket pocket.

By this time I was both mentally and physically drained from Joe's unknown character. Yet, when we spent the weekend over at my parents' home Joe would still torment me. For example, once he burst into the bathroom where I was washing my hair and I had taken my watch and rings off. Joe grabbed my black stone ring that my parents had bought me and threw it hard into the bath. As a result, the stone came out of the ring setting and the ring itself was badly damaged. I cried so much that my parents wanted to know what on earth was going on. Joe got in first by saying he was under a lot of stress from work and his family which was reflecting on our relationship. Joe sounded convincing, producing crocodile tears, and my parents believed him.

A rare opportunity arose for my mother and me to be alone

and I opened up and told her everything about the beatings, unexplained strange happenings and how Joe's family treated me. A breakthrough came in the form of my sister Eileen and her husband inviting Joe and myself to stay with them in Salisbury. Within a month arrangements were being made with my older sister and her family for Joe and me to start a new and hopefully a happy life together. During my time at Parkside I took strength from my spirit guides. Without them I would not have got through the uncomfortable circumstances. Past events had made me a stronger person. Saying goodbye to Joe's family and closing the front door on Parkside was a wonderful feeling of freedom. When I looked up at the landing window for the last time I am convinced I saw the image of a huge man grinning at me. I gave one final shudder to shake the negative energy and replace it quickly with positive thoughts. However, I could never see a future with Joe because we never spoke of starting a family. Maybe that was a blessing in disguise or was it spiritual insight on my part?

12

The Friary

The Friary is the name of a housing estate that is situated near the internationally renowned Salisbury cathedral which dates back to 1220 and was finished in 1258. The spire is the tallest one in England at 404 feet high. This housing estate is large in size and consists of a mixture of dwellings such as houses, flats and maisonettes. My sister Eileen and her husband Andrew, with their two young sons, lived in a three-bedroom maisonette. The difference between Eileen's maisonette and the previous one I used to live in was that she had a public lift and stairs whereas I only had a flight of stairs. The height of these buildings was about four floors and there were about ten family residences in a uniform row. The entire Friary was one of many council estates. However, Salisbury cathedral dominated the town because if a new business was found not suitable for whatever reason the council would not agree to it opening up. Before Joe and I moved over to England my sister's husband had enquired about a job in a local bakery with Joe in mind. As a result, an interview was arranged for Joe's arrival. When we arrived in Salisbury it felt like we were on holiday. Instead we were there to settle into a new lifestyle. Luckily Joe got the job and started work straight away. My sister worked for a company making diving suits and even though it was only part time she was able to get employment for me as a sewing machinist which meant both Joe and I had money coming on a regular basis. Nevertheless, things were still not right between Joe and me. I found out he was usually at the bookies instead of being at work but still taking my share of the money when I thought we were saving up to buy a house. Every time we looked at properties Joe never really seemed to be interested and only wanted to go for a drink. Suddenly I was starting to feel like a failure to myself, my family and my friends. I really did feel alone because I was trying to put a brave face to show to everyone that everything was going to turn out well. The only one it was going well for was Joe because he was still physically beating me but I had no more energy to fight back. I had now learnt the art of covering up black eyes with plenty of eye shadow and wearing appropriate clothing to hide the bruising. The situation was not looking too good. In addition, Joe's plan of applying mental persecution towards me was working. From nowhere he would just come towards me chanting stupid things till I covered my ears trying to block out his behaviour. I began to realise he was a liar as well because on one occasion the factory where I worked gave everyone a half day off due to completing an order on time. Myself and two other girls decided to walk through the parkland and who should I see but Joe kissing and cuddling on the grass with a young sixteen- or seventeen-year-old girl. I was hardly going to point out to my companions what I had just witnessed. I plucked up courage and confronted Joe about what I had seen in the park. Joe tried to deny it but then showed me pictures of them together taken earlier that day in a photo booth. At that point I felt the strength in my right hand rising up and before I knew it I hit Joe for the very first time. This was only the second time I can remember ever having a physical anger outburst since I was a child. However, I finished up getting a good thrashing from Joe. It is true what people say, violence breeds violence. At night I would lie in our bedroom which was at the front of the maisonette feeling mentally tired and try to go to sleep. However, I was woken up by strange dark shapes hovering in front of me. I sensed fear because the room was full of these dark outlines. I tried to pull bedcovers over my face but I was just paralysed with terror. Also, as quick as the dark shapes appeared suddenly they would just disappear. Furthermore, since the sighting of these strange dark shapes they began to visit me on a regular basis. They would come very near to me but somehow I had overcome my hidden fear which was replaced by a comforting feeling. Were they my spirit guides trying to protect me? Since my experience with the dark shapes strange things began to happen around the maisonette even to the point that my sister and her family started to notice. Their heating was a form of storage heaters situated in certain rooms but for some weird reason some of the heaters would not function on their programmed time settings. It was as if someone had tampered with the controls. Alarm clocks and washing machines all stopped functioning plus various items went missing but turned up later in different places. Everywhere I went in and around the Friary it felt like I had an invisible protector with me. Looking back I believe that my psychic ability was becoming stronger around me but I was still ignorant about my true identity.

Somehow, I was being directed towards places of new employment. For example, as I walked past a shop just off the town centre called 'Plumbs' which sold items such as bedding and stretch furniture covers, I noticed a sign advertising a job vacancy for a part-time sales assistant. Next thing I knew I was being interviewed and got the job within twenty-four hours. This new job began to give me new confidence and this led me to making new friendships. Furthermore, I noticed that as I was working in the centre of Salisbury all the buildings felt like they would come alive when I entered them. For example, the shop I worked in was fully modernised but you cannot take away the original foundations. At times

I sensed a male energy around the top floor of the shop which was used for storing the stock. If you switched off the light precisely half an hour later that light would be turned back on. Looking back when I was left in the shop on my own the spotlights would just go off and sometimes the cash till would not operate properly. Was this happening because spirit energies had found a way of communicating with someone like me?

One time one of girls who worked in the shop invited everyone to a nightclub to celebrate her birthday. It was in a converted manor house called the Grange that also served as a local hotel. I was really looking forward to going out with the girls because I never got the opportunity to get dressed up. From the moment I arrived at the Grange I fell in love with the place and its atmosphere. I felt I would love to have the opportunity of walking up the sweeping staircase that led to the numerous rooms upstairs. I noticed a lovely old gentleman sat in a large leather chair by the imposing fireplace. He smiled and I nodded politely back. I asked my friends what they thought of the nice old man just sitting watching the world go by and to my astonishment they turned round and said what man? I immediately blamed it on swallowing my first drink too quickly but I know what I had seen. In fact, after many visits to the Grange I would always acknowledge my sweet old gentleman from the spirit world. Also, I had started to sense things before the events actually happened. For example, I had a really strong hunch that my parents were coming over to visit from Ireland and I told my sister. Two weeks later my father turned up with the intention of moving the rest of the family over to England. After long periods of house hunting eventually a home was purchased from a couple who wanted to move back to Leighton Buzzard. In the meantime my father noticed many changes in me; how tired and thin I had got. I could not carry on the false pretence that things between Joe and me were fine.

70

Indeed, I told my father everything and he said changes would be made once they moved over to England. An agreement was made between the vendor of the Laverstock property and my father that Joe and I could move in while the contracts were being exchanged. Also, when the moving day came the property would not be left empty. After my father had returned home to Ireland, Joe and I were preparing to leave the Friary when I had a vision about Joe leaving me for good. A voice or thought was telling me to 'abide your time my child, freedom is only a little distance away'. When I have a vision or think I hear voices it feels like I am in a trance-like state for only a split second but actually it seems longer to me personally. Maybe all these strange happenings were due to the fact that the Friary was built very close to Salisbury cathedral, a building that held an array of mixed spiritual energies.

13

Laverstock

Laverstock is an area which lies on the outskirts of Salisbury and consists of an array of houses, small industrial units and a local pub called the Duck which is tucked up a lane behind our neighbouring properties. It was strange living with complete strangers and not your own family. In fact, we only had three weeks with the Smyths before they moved to Leighton Buzzard to be closer to their family. On the other hand this meant Joe and I would have at least four weeks on our own before my parents plus younger sister came from Northern Ireland to England. Our new home in Laverstock was built around 1930. It was a semi-detached set in a cul-de-sac. It had a pleasant walled front garden, a driveway and a garage. The front entrance greeted you with a lovely floor-tiled porch and once you entered the front door the hallway was spacious with a flight of stairs to the left plus one doorway leading to the lounge and a door opposite leading to the kitchen. The lounge had a comfy feeling to it as there was an open fireplace. The dining section would once have been separated by dividing doors so my mother put some curtains up to soften the entrance. Also in the dining room there were French doors that brought you out to the patio area and a long garden plus a greenhouse. From the dining room was a door into a kitchen of average size, but big enough to house a table plus chairs. Also there was an old-style pantry because years ago not everyone could afford fridges and pantries were included to keep food cooler and to last longer. At the top of the stairs was a window. The first door led to my parents' bedroom which was at the front of the house. This room never really did look bright but again I was comfortable with the feel of it. As you turned left and walked along the landing the door on the left was the family bathroom which was big enough for this size of property. On the opposite side of the hallway was the room that Joe and I shared. This room was the brightest of all the bedrooms but the wallpaper was unusual because it was a Sanderson design with big Scottish-type thistles which was appropriate for what had and would take place between Joe and I. This room overlooked the back gardens of our neighbours as did my sister's room but her room was the box bedroom and had a dull image to it. Part of me was secretly praying for some sort of a miracle to happen to sort out the problem between Joe and myself. Someone in heaven was listening and my prayers were answered but not before I had endured a number of physical batterings. As the Smyths's furniture moved out at last I was reunited with our furniture which had been in storage all this time. Some of the furniture we sold before we left Ireland and only kept the basic items. My sister Eileen and her hubby invited Joe and I up to what was to become my local pub, the Duck. The evening started out very pleasant but then it started to take on a nasty turn for the worst. The four of us were involved in a game of darts which everyone was enjoying except for Joe. I was sat by my sister waiting for our turn to play when all of a sudden I felt an excruciating pain coming from my right kneecap. I let out a squeal of both shock and pain and heard my sister saying, 'Don't look down.' Unknown to me Joe had used my leg for target practice and had thrown a dart deliberately aimed at my kneecap. I could not get angry at this person any more. Nothing surprised me where Joe was concerned. Joe was determined to continue his strategy of abuse towards me and our next door neighbour revealed to my parents how she had heard me sobbing on numerous occasions through the walls of our home. On the day my family arrived from Ireland Joe attacked me fifteen minutes before I heard my father turn his key in the front door. It was a relief to have the warmth, love and security of my family around me because I did yearn for them. As a result of my family beginning a new life away from the troubles of Northern Ireland my parents approached me and asked if Joe and I were getting on any better. I could no longer hold back and my emotions got the better of me and I told them exactly what my married life was like with Joe. We had only been married thirteen months when Joe departed to return to his native home town of Portadown. Joe's family tried to make my life hell because I had filed for a divorce and they tried to obstruct the situation. However, I did get my divorce plus Joe's life was short lived; ironically he ended up living in my home town Lurgan with his new partner. Nevertheless Joe always had a fascination with fire and it was this that eventually killed him. Joe was smoking in bed and must have fallen asleep and his cigarette must have set fire to the property because Joe was announced dead on arrival at the hospital. At last I was released from Joe's mental and physical torture which was one journey that I had lived to survive but it was the faith in my guardian angels plus spirit guides that assisted me through the torment of one angered man. With Joe out of my life I was at last able to construct and rebuild a new life for myself. Firstly I was offered the position of full-time sales assistant in a shop. Secondly, it was at this property that my spirit sightings began to become more frequent plus my psychic vibes were becoming much stronger. For example, Fran my manageress and I began to go out socially to night clubs in and around the Salisbury area. One night we decided to go to a hotel called The High Post, as most hotels had adjoining night clubs. I always felt very agitated every time we went there for a night out because something would not let me settle. On this particular evening they had a disco plus a group, and a national Radio 1 DJ was making an appearance. It was a busy evening as Fran and I eventually found a tiny gap at the bar so we stayed there and a group of five guys came and stood beside us. For no apparent reason I started chatting about the group and what type of songs we might expect from them. Suddenly one of the five guys turned around and said he could guarantee a wonderful evening of good entertainment because he was the lead singer of the group. First and foremost I was realising how my spiritual pathway had developed a sense of humour by planting some thoughts in my mind plus seeing them materialise within a matter of moments was very hard for me to acknowledge. I apologised to the guy for thinking my thoughts out loud when he introduced himself as Pete. We got chatting like a house on fire and Pete said he would dedicate the first song to me and I was to listen to the lyrics. As the group ventured onto the stage Fran and I positioned ourselves near the stage area to hear this first song. Funnily it was titled 'Heaven Must be Missing an Angel'. Strange but true was this a sign that an angel has been sent down to earth with the task of directing and educating a petite Irish Colleen heavenly ways. Boy, do they know what a huge task they have taken on? When Pete was playing at various gigs in and around the Salisbury area we would arrange to see each other. I never looked upon it as a relationship, only a platonic friendship because personally I was keeping male relationships at an arm's length. However, one night after a gig Pete and I decided to stop off at what is renowned as an area for courting couples called Old Sarum Castle. Old Sarum Castle is an Iron Age fortress reused by the Romans, Saxons and Normans before growing into a flourishing settlement in medieval England. I had never been there before until that particular evening. Driving along the cinder track towards the castle mounds I sensed a complete mood change of panic and unease, and the temperature dropped instantly. As Pete circled round the car park looking for a vacant spot I really did not want to be there. Just as Pete stopped the engine I had the feeling that our car was surrounded with spirit energies from the past. Pete asked if I wanted to walk around the castle grounds but I explained that I was not feeling too good which he accepted and so we left the remaining courting couples. On our way out of the castle I turned around and I am sure I saw fires burning plus silhouettes of soldiers guarding and protecting their beloved castle. I have never returned to Old Sarum Castle nor do I have any future plans to do so.

Fran my boss was leaving Plumbs to live in Wales to be closer to her fiancée, Tony. This meant that I had first refusal of the manageress job which would be great for me because I never had the chance before to work within a team plus myself leading a group of people. Life for me began to take on a different role spiritually because my mother started to become involved with doing more readings for people other than family members. I started psychically becoming more aware of my spiritual intuition. My mystical senses began to work overtime allowing me to reach my sixth sense without really knowing what I was doing. I remember coming out of the family bathroom which was just opposite my bedroom when I called out. Both my parents dashed upstairs and my sister came from her bedroom to see what the commotion was. What I had encountered was a huge bright light or shape of something that surrounded the landing area. This unknown energy stayed around for about five minutes and at first I thought someone had parked on our driveway and left their headlights on. When I looked out of the window there was nothing there. It was then that I realised I had stumbled upon something not of this earth plane. I explained to my family what I had seen and it was only then that my mother actually admitted I had the psychic gift. Also she explained that as a mother she wanted to protect me from the unknown pathway the gift might lead me to. Only then did my mother decided to pass on her psychic knowledge to me. If truth be told I really did feel worthy of learning my mother's psychic ability because I knew her reputation as a card reader. One night when Fran and I went to the Grange I knew I was going to meet a guy. I did not know what he would look like, just that a meeting would take place. Salisbury was a garrison town due to the neighbouring army camps. Next thing I knew a soldier sat down by me and started talking to me. His name was Steve and he was from the Yorkshire area and was stationed in Bulford camp with an infantry regiment. Steve was very pleasant but all evening I was trying to convince myself that he fancied my friend Fran instead of me. Steve and I met a short time before my family decided to return to Northern Ireland due to the fact that my father's parents where getting no younger. Also Carol my older sister was expecting her first child. In addition, a huge house had just come up for sale opposite to Carol and Jim's property. This property was called White Gables. I decided to remain in Salisbury because my divorce was only halfway through so it was arranged that I should stay with my sister Eileen and her family. However, once my family moved back to Ireland I did feel homesick. When I went over to visit my family I decided to move back to Ireland. Within two months I was planning my return trip. I handed in my notice at work and I was sad at giving up the chance of making a career within Plumbs. However, my life path was being pulled in a new direction, but did it include Steve? Strange but true at the same time I decided to make the break from England Steve received orders to take part in peacekeeping duties in Zimbabwe. Was this the work of the spirits? I said all my farewells to my sister plus her family and friends but I was returning to a different part of Northern Ireland, Belfast. Both Belfast and I were strangers to each other so what lay ahead of me was anybody's guess.

14

White Gables

White Gables is located in an area called Hannahstown situated on the west side of Belfast. The area borders onto the neighbouring countryside. Hannahstown is situated halfway up a mountain face locally known as the Black Mountain because of the big dark boulders protruding through the odd pieces of grass. The Black Mountain has other areas of interest such as a stone quarry, home for the roaming livestock, plus the all important communication aerials for TV, radio and telephone broadcasting transmitters. However, White Gables took its name from the fact that the house has four large gable ends and the property was always painted white. White Gables was a house that had much diverse spiritual energy, both positive and negative. This could be connected to the history of the property which included a violent murder, natural death but most of all the birth of children. The above-mentioned all happened in my lifetime. God knows what events had previously taken place. White Gables was just parallel to where Carol's little house stood, which was very basic and did not have any bath or shower facilities or central heating, all important for a new baby. Carol noticed a For Sale sign outside White Gables and on impulse got the details of the property and sent them for my parents' approval. It was decided between the two families that White Gables was big enough for them to live under the same roof. My father gave Carol power of attorney to act on his behalf to purchase the next family home. Before our families joined the list of ownership, White Gables had belonged to a wealthy landowner who built the property to suit his family needs plus his business, which was quarrying for stone. Our family only know of information about the last two owners from people who have lived and grown up on the Hannahstown Road. Daniel Garner lived in this magnificence residence during the height of the Northern Ireland troubles. It was at this property that Daniel met his fate by opening his front door to his unknown executioner. It was soon after that terrible incident that White Gables was searching for a new owner. This came in the form of the Armstrong family who had a pet shop business. A For Sale sign was put up for a third time. Maybe White Gables was starting to give signs of discontent between people who moved in and those spiritual energies that already live there. The next residents crossing the threshold were the Ferris and Murray families. This was the beginning of a loving relationship between a house and my sister Carol. White Gables stands in about sixteen acres of ground and has various outbuildings. A solid steel structure called the breaker protrudes from the side of the mountain because the property also at one time owned the quarry which is still producing stone and gravel. Other buildings include a stable block and a red brick building to house the proud landowner's coach. White Gables dates back to the early Victorian times and to this day you can still see their craftsmanship and traits, for example, beautiful large coach lights scattered around the pillars or fixed onto the buildings on the perimeter of the property, also wrought iron fencing and garden gates, magnificent carpentry skills and Adam-style fireplaces, not forgetting the wonderful layout of the gardens. Around 1957 a new extension was built onto the property to bring the kitchen into more modern times.

Both families were delighted with their purchase. Not long after my family moved in it was time for me to fly over and see this grand building for myself. My sister Carol met me at the Belfast International Airport and we were both very excited at seeing each other but at the same time I was thinking, what will I think of White Gables? Love it or hate it? The journey through the neighbouring countryside was beautiful and peaceful until Carol broke the silence by informing me, 'Not long now.' However, she did detour a little of the way before I realised we were in the middle of a housing estate and Carol wanted to show me the eaves of White Gables peeking through the high screen of trees. Shrubs and hedgerows protected the huge imposing property, which could only be approached via a sweeping driveway that brings you to a huge area my family nicknamed the yard. Straight away strange sensations took place within me. Why do I get into such a state I began to question myself, because these circumstances were becoming more common. As I got out of the car both my parents welcomed me with words to the effect of, 'Wherever we are there will always be a room for you. Welcome to your new home.' At that precise moment I remembered surveying the yard area. There were other people there but who were they? They were dressed from a different era from us. I just put it down to tiredness and the emotional side of being reunited with my family. To the left side of the yard was a high slope covered with lots of trees and shrubs all growing at very odd angles. This area has always been renowned for the wildlife that would constantly roam around. Beyond this high gradient was the domineering quarry. You would feel underground movement in the house or loud exploding bangs when the quarry workers were blasting. To the right-hand side of the sweeping driveway immediately before you approached the house was a large vegetable garden. I always sensed that there was someone else in the garden with you and you were never alone. Carol would agree with that statement but it was never a horrible feeling, just that you sensed someone else was with you.

81

Immediately after the house was another huge garden that had pathways leading off in all different directions. In the centre of the garden was a large square pond about four feet deep, full of carp. Carol had actually seen old photographs of White Gables and the surrounding ground as it portrayed the full beauty of what was once an imposing property. It was crying out for some tender loving care. For example, the pond was missing a big stone fountain which would have stood proudly in the centre with water streaming out from various outlets. The gardens had a breathtaking array of flowers and shrubs but unfortunately as time went by the two previous owners lost interest and the weeds slowly took over. One or more gardeners would have been employed along with various members of staff to help and maintain the upkeep of what was once a splendid family residence. I sensed a sad remorseful feeling when I walked around the little overgrown pathways. I wanted to enjoy what beauty was left in this ornamental garden but at the same I felt that it was my fault it had degenerated over the years. Was I really sensing the emotions of previous spiritual energies who had. attended these fine-looking grounds? I was extremely intrigued and could not wait to enter this elegant dwelling. The property had a very strange back to front appearance because the back door was the first entrance you saw from the driveway. The front door was at the opposite side of the house facing the main road. I noticed that the property contained a quantity of various-sized windows which meant there were a lot of rooms. There was a large glass porchway with beautiful black and white floor tiles and on either side of the walls a trellis for flower pots, etc. I had mixed feelings at this point because part of me was saying this large detached property was compelling and homely. On the other hand, I felt inner fear rising within me as if I had to be on my guard, but against what? Opposite the front door was another full length glass door leading into a large hallway with a further four doors leading off in different directions. There was a single flight of stairs leading to the various bedrooms and family bathroom. The hallway straight away gave me a sensation that something horrible or nasty had happened there; none of the family members including myself would hang about there. In fact, the only time we used the hall was for going upstairs or going to the front door.

Not long after my arrival Carol explained to me that one of the previous owners had been murdered in the hallway when he opened the front door. This event had taken place in the early 1970s when the troubles in Northern Ireland were at their height. I always felt the hairs on the back of my neck stand up when I looked at the mirror which reflected towards the front door because you could sense someone was standing behind you and it was not a nice feeling. The first of the doorways leading off the hallway brought you to a generous sized cloakroom which included a toilet and hand basin plus a coat rail. I never liked using that particular loo because I had an experience of a strange kind. I popped in to use the toilet and locked the door as normal. However, after I unlocked the door it still would not open and it felt like someone was holding the door handle to try and prevent me from getting out. In the end I shouted and my father set me free. My father put it down as another one of his jobs to add to his list but I know someone or an unknown energy was holding onto the door handle. The second doorway brought me into a large, bright and airy room which had two massive bay windows. This room would have been called the great room in Victorian times. I noticed the warm colour of the maple flooring which was springy as you walked on it. This type of flooring was also used in the hallway and dining room. Again it was highlighting how wealthy the original owner was. In the centre of this room stood an elegant Adam-style fireplace which dominated the room but in a very pleasant way. I felt cold when I entered the great room but not frightened. I was intrigued with this location because unbeknown to me at a later stage I would find myself going into this room and just sitting quietly alone, or was I? In fact, this room gave me the same sensations as North Street's front sitting room; very strange, I thought. The third door led you into a room that would have been called the morning room in Victorian times. This room was the smallest of all the first-floor rooms. In a way, I always felt overcome with heat or a stuffy feeling like you had just entered a room with a blazing fire. Last but not least was the fourth door which brought you into a long but kind of wide area with built-in cupboards on either side. A huge archway was at the opposite end with three doors. One brought you back into the large sitting room. The second led to the dining room. The third brought you to the pantry because in Victorian times there was no fridge. Our family named this dark passage the lobby. No natural light ever came directly into this location. Everyone had a weird experience or two in the lobby area. We called the lobby the whispering hallway because all you could hear was low whispers even though you were the only person there. The voices of people who had passed over to the spirit world would constantly be heard in the whispering hallway. The lobby housed the servants' bells that would have been buzzed from the various rooms in the house by the master or mistress. Maybe those whisperings were servants cursing about having to attend to their employers?

From the lobby area, I entered the dining room which my parents used as their living room. This room had a lovely atmosphere of warmth, love and gaiety. Also, it had a lovely bay window which was fitting for my mother's most loved ornaments and pictures of family members. From this window you could see the dividing hedgerow which separated the vegetable garden from the house. In this room I had the feeling of coming home to Ireland for good so there and then I decided White Gables might be my future home too. However,

I sometimes got the sensation that my family's living room was very active with spiritual energies because you would get the occasional cold draught by you or you would see the outline of a figure close by you. Opposite to the dining room was the doorway to what the Victorians called the family room. In fact, this room became Carol and Jim's living room. This room had really high ceilings and a window recess that must have had a window seat because this area had beautiful dark wood panelling. Once again I felt very at home in this room because it had a lovely welcoming feeling. Also, this room overlooked the ornamental pond and garden which meant that wherever you were in the room the garden was always in view. Finally, we come to the new part of the house which was the kitchen area. I never really felt at home in this part of the house. There was something close by that I just could not explain. The atmosphere was always that of being in a freezer and again strange happenings occurred there such as things or items going missing. Another door brought you into what was once the old kitchen but my family used it as a utility area. Also, there was a separate toilet. Quarry tiles covered the kitchen, utility and toilet floor areas. In addition, high up on the utility wall was an electricity power supply. However, this power supply was very unusual because it had what is known as three phases of electricity. Power could be turned on either in one, two or all three areas of the property. The owner of the property ruled the use of the electricity because it was seen as a luxury. From the utility room was the back door which looked out to the mountain slope. Once I started to ascend the only single flight of stairs that would lead you to five bedrooms, a separate toilet and bathroom I immediately sensed that these stairs had other spiritual energies using them too. At the top were five doorways. To my right was the separate toilet and the next door was the bathroom. Both toilet and bathroom suite were fine examples of Victorian porcelain with big wide handbasins with taps that you would find in reclamation yards in present times. The taps had the logo BWC which stands for Belfast Water Commissioners. Also, this property would have been the first one in the area to have a modern flush toilet. Next door along was a bedroom that faced onto the main road and this was my parents' room. This room had a lovely fireplace with a push button at the side for servants' attendance. I liked this room because it had a nice secure feel to it. Was it because the room belonged to my parents or could it have been the spiritual energy welcoming me? The room after that was Carol and Jim's bedroom. This was the largest of all the bedrooms and had a lovely fireplace with a servant's button. I had become aware of how cold this room was but Carol put it down to being a large house to keep warm. On the other hand, why should I be the only one reacting strangely towards the various rooms? The last door of the landing area was a real surprise because you walked into an average-sized room with no fireplace. This part of the building had a totally different feel. I knew that I was trespassing on someone else's territory, but whose? The room had a creepy feeling and I was hoping my mother did not want me to sleep there. What a lovely surprise as we entered the next room. What a weird and wonderful bedroom. Was it used for other purposes? Straight away I connected to this room. The room had a small narrow hallway entrance with wooden shelves to the left hand side and a small but perfectly formed cast iron fireplace. This room may have doubled up as a bedroom-cum-dressing room. Most of the eaves was blocked off and used as storage space. There was only a small window which let in natural light but the room looked much brighter than the previous one considering they both faced onto the mountain slope. The warm feeling from this room gave me a lovely experience of overwhelming emotion; I was sharing a brief moment with the spiritual past residents who no longer walk this earth. At last my mother said, 'Pauline, this room will always be known as your bedroom. While I am still alive there will always be a room for you.' I was really taken aback by my mother's statement or was it the emotions of my new spiritual friends that nearly brought me to tears? Finally, we came to the last bedroom. This room could only be reached by entering the previous two bedrooms. This room belonged to my younger sister Orla. My God, I never knew a room could feel so freezing; it was like something had walked over my grave. I shuddered and you could plainly see the goosebumps had risen on my arms. This room I sensed was trapped in time but in what way I did not know. The room gave you the feeling of entering a chapel instead of a bedroom because the ceiling was shaped like one you would expect to find in a church. There was a cast iron fireplace at one end and a small window at the opposite end of the room which was positioned at the front of the house. Yet again, either side of the room had built-in storage space. The energy in this room was not as nice as my bedroom so my inclination was telling me to make sure that particular door was always kept shut.

I enjoyed my vacation with my family and meeting their new friends. However, when I returned to England the truth was I felt homesick and decided to go back to Northern Ireland for good to be in the bosom of my family. On my return to White Gables I viewed the house differently because this was not a passing visit. In fact, this was to be my new home. The move back to Ireland had another side because I was not sure if I wanted to get married to Steve. I decided to come back to Ireland to give myself some breathing space and to contemplate what my future had to offer. I settled down to being part of family life again. It was a great feeling, having both my parents fussing over me and making me feel secure. Indeed, after my past experiences of men my confidence was extremely low. The house began to have an effect on me. For example, the areas I would not linger around were the whispering hallway, the hall and the first and second bedroom either side of my bedroom. I sensed that I was being watched or spoken to but no one was there. I had sensations of feeling cold when everyone else was feeling warm. I actually thought I was going mad. However, every time I sensed a strange experience it was a male energy that had a strong character. Was I running away from my psychic ability, I often asked myself.

Carol gave birth to a daughter. About the same time my father's parents developed a crisis because my grandfather had developed diabetes and my frail old grandmother was not up to looking after them both. As a result, my grandfather went into a residential care home and my granny came to live at White Gables. It was decided that granny should have my bedroom because it would be the warmest room due to the fact that the living room below always had a fire. My worst nightmare came when I was told I would sleep in the first of the adjoining bedrooms. To be honest I ended up most nights sleeping in my younger sister's bedroom. Remember this was the chapel-shaped bedroom where it felt like being in a freezer. At night when we got ready for bed it was always a race to see who was going to switch off the light because none of us wanted to move around in the dark. When all the family had retired to bed and the house was locked up the floorboards would squeak. Orla's door handle would turn and we would call out to see if it was granny who needed us. But no one was there. Furthermore, my sister's room would develop a hazy or smoky effect and then little lights would appear from nowhere. We both got up out of bed and went to the window to see if anyone was out there shining lights up to the bedrooms but we could not find any reason why this should be happening. The strange lights did not come from any passing cars. Were these bright little lights so-called orbs which can be described as the beginning of a spiritual energy trying to manifest itself? All I know is that it frightened the life out of both of us. Again, it felt like the old experiences at Shore Road. No one would take you seriously, even my mother was a bit quiet and would not fully comment on the matter.

One day my granny was sitting in our living room and she fancied a cup of tea so I offered to make her one. I was just coming through the whispering hallway to approach the kitchen when I saw a woman dressed in Victorian clothes enter the kitchen before me. Well, I was stunned. I did not want to alarm my grandmother by screaming but I had to find out what was going on. I plucked up my courage and asked granny what type of clothes would the original female owners have worn? Granny described the lady's outfit exactly as I had seen her and when I told granny the reason why I wanted to know, she said, 'Oh sweetheart, she is always around because she is the lady of the house. We are her tenants, she will not harm you.' So my granny could see spirits too! I was not alone, nor going out of my head. As a result of my sighting in the whispering hallway my granny and I would often chat about paranormal themes. Granny could actually read the cinders in the fire and one night my family were all sitting in the living room when my granny began her skill of scribing in the glowing cinders of the fire. However, what my granny did not realise was she had foreseen her own death. The scenario she was describing was correct down to the description of the ambulance driver and the paramedics. Granny previously had a slight stoke but her speech was not affected. However, she developed a nasty chest-type infection and because of her age my parents thought it was best to send for the doctor who said granny would be better off in hospital. The hospital was quite satisfied with granny's progress and the doctor decided to sign her release papers. My grandmother was returned to her loving family and the house she called home. On the evening of my grandmother's return I had the most uncomfortable feeling.

I just cannot explain or try to put it into words. For one thing, I knew that I could not sleep that evening so my younger sister Orla and I decided we would sleep down in our living room. Our parents said it was okay and they wanted granny to have a good night's sleep even though my mother wanted to sleep in a chair by granny's bedside but granny was stubborn and said she would have a good night's sleep in her own wee bed. So all the family said their goodnights to each other and most of all we were pleased to see granny cracking some of her jokes which meant she was on the road to recovery, or so the family thought. My sister and I chatted way into the early hours of the morning. Dozing off I could hear a tapping coming from above me; not sure if I was dreaming I sat up and listened for as long as I could but nothing happened. Next morning as part of his routine since our grandmother came to stay at White Gables, my father would make tea and toast to bring upstairs for his mother. Unknown to my father his mother had passed away in her sleep. In fact, my father thought she was in a deep sleep after her experience of being in hospital just twenty four hours earlier and then he felt her pulse and realised she was dead. After my father got over the initial shock of his mother's death he roused the rest of the family and broke the sad news. It was then that I remembered the tapping noise. Did my granny want to let me know she had departed to a heavenly place? I went up to my grandmother's bedroom. I could not get over seeing her lying on her side, both hands tucked under her chin in what seemed a very deep peaceful sleep. There were no signs of her being distressed. My grandmother really enjoyed her time at White Gables because it gave her the opportunity to spend time with her son and his family.

Into the family was born the fourth generation of girls. There is a saying in Ireland, 'As one comes into this world one leaves the world.' Is this true or is it just a phrase? However, Carol's daughter, now in her mid-twenties, recalls an incident when there was a group of friends sitting in the morning room when my niece's boyfriend went white and claimed he had seen an old lady in a long nightdress with her hair in a long plait. The image of the lady was going upstairs and then she just disappeared. This young man had encountered the spirit of my grandmother who was still enjoying her ties with White Gables. However, the young man to this day does not like being left alone in any of the rooms.

After my grandmother's death the house took on a different kind of feeling. I moved back into my old bedroom with mixed emotions at first but I always recall my mother saying, 'It's not the dead you should be frightened of but the living.' Looking back I realised just how much I loved and missed my grandmother because she was the only one that I had ever known due to the fact that my grandmother on my mother's side of the family passed away before I was born.

Family life at White Gables began to settle back down to normality or I thought it had until a particular event. This incident occurred when I offered to baby-sit for Carol and her husband because since the birth of their daughter plus my grandmother's death they had not had a social night out. Therefore, everyone jumped at the idea of having an evening out and I stayed to look after my niece who was also my god-daughter. After everyone had gone out for the evening I settled down to watch TV as my niece was safely sleeping when suddenly the room temperature dropped to that of a freezing winter's day. In addition, there were loud noises coming from the kitchen area of crockery being rattled or moved around. I was absolutely petrified but luckily my niece slept through the incident without waking up. Once my family returned home I went into the kitchen and nothing was out of place, so who was playing with my spiritual mind? In fact, these effects plus a lot more incidents often occurred but no one would ever discuss or even speak about it. My family would past odd comments about minor events that happened around the property but no one had ever taken the issue further to find out who where the spiritual energies that roamed around the property. I tried to disengage myself from this property because I felt that White Gables was trying to take over my sanity or perhaps I was denying my gifted pathway? In fact, I was never sure if I loved or hated White Gables. Steve and I had kept corresponding since I returned to Northern Ireland. As a result, we decided to get married once Steve returned from his tour of duty in Zimbabwe. Therefore, I was busy preparing my departure back to England. My parents were accompanying me to attend my wedding. I arrived at White Gables by entering the property through the front door and strangely enough I left the house by the same door.

15

Edmonton House

My return journey to England involved crossing by boat to
arrive at Liverpool docks before embarking on a long train
ride to Salisbury. I was really pleased that my parents had
accompanied me on this long jaunt. Just before the train had
reached our destination my mother enquired if I actually
wanted to get married to Steve. I replied, 'Yes this is what
I want to do.' However, I suddenly thought, did my mother
take delivery of a spiritual insight about my forthcoming
marriage or was it purely a hunch that she should ask such
a question? Maybe my parents were feeling apprehensive
because up until that point they had only spoken to Steve on
the telephone and this was going to be their first meeting.
As the train pulled into the station platform I saw Steve
standing there and believe it or not I sensed a pulling towards
my emotions of 'don't go down that avenue' but I turned
my back on my intuition once again much to my cost, as
you shall see later. Steve was extremely pleased and excited
at meeting my family plus the fact that they would be staying
at the home of my sister Eileen. Married quarters had just
been released to Steve two days before we arrived from
Ireland. It was a ground-floor two-bedroom flat but Steve
thought I would be put off that our new house number was
going to be number thirteen. I was born on Friday the thirteenth
so it did not bother me one bit. As we piled into Steve's car
and headed towards Bulford army camp a feeling of panic

or confusion was growing within me. Our block of flats was the one at the end of what can only be portrayed as a concrete jungle. Due to the fact it was a weekend I found out that army camps go quite lifeless over this period due to exercises taking place or lads being on the drink the night before. As we entered the block of flats we had to descend down a flight of stairs and turn left. Number thirteen was staring me in the face. A sudden sensation overcame me and I knew that I was about to embark on another new level of my life-path. Steve unlocked the door which brought you into a short hallway with a doorway at one end. This was a storage area. There was a second longer hallway with five doors leading off it. The first door on the left was a bedroom but I sensed a cold feeling as I entered this room. However, the second bedroom was much larger in size and brighter in outlook. This would have to be our bedroom. A door on the opposite side of the hallway brought you into a bathroom which was small in size and had no window which meant the light had to be used at all times plus an extractor fan would automatically come on with the light. Finally, the last two remaining doors led into a warm oblong lounge decorated in earthy colours. All married quarters come fully furnished and equipped with household essentials. We made do with the army-issued furniture for the first few months before we started buying our own bits and pieces. Lastly was an L-shaped kitchen/diner which could be approached from the long hallway door or from the lounge. Where the lounge window was there was a door close by which led you out to an open plan area. Prior to my return journey, Steve had been to Salisbury register office to set a date for our wedding, which we decided would be on the fourteenth of April because I was born on the thirteenth of that month and Steve on the fifteenth. I should have seen this as a sign from above that future confrontation lay ahead of me. Again I overlooked precious signs, being so wrapped up in settling down in a new home and of course the pre-wedding plans. However, not long after came another omen in the form of who should have collected the flowers for the wedding because no one really chatted about whose job it was to collect them. How could this happen on such an important day? As it is custom for the bride and groom not to see each other on their wedding night my sister Eileen invited my parents and myself to stay with them. Steve and members of his family who had made the journey down to Bulford stayed in our flat. We planned a small buffet for family members plus people who were attending the wedding. As I was nearly ready I just could not get desperately excited that I was about to get married. I recall a memory of lying on the bed dressed in my wedding garments and my father came in. We had a one to one talk but I honestly do not remember the exact conversation. It was only then I realised no one had taken on the job of picking up the flowers from the florists and then panic set in: was this how my new life was going to be, living in trepidation? After the wedding ceremony and mini-wedding reception we said our farewells and headed down to London for a couple of nights at the Ex-Servicemen's Club. This was an establishment purely for people who had served or were still serving in the forces, plus it was an inexpensive way to stay in London. I do not remember one encapsulating memory of my honeymoon. Once we returned to Bulford and my parents were heading back to Ireland I realised just how lonely and cold this new home actually was. I detested having to walk past parade grounds, seeing tanks plus anything to do with the military. What was happening to me? Was I homesick or could it have anything to do with my past experience of being a soldier and getting shot? I decided to try and settle down to being an army wife so I got myself a job working for the Co-op in their wine and spirit department in the neighbouring village. Steve and I decided to save my wages towards buying a house because he had been in the army since he was sixteen years old and wanted to settle down in civilian street. In the meantime I became friendly with another soldier's wife whose husband was in the same regiment as Steve. Sally was the daughter of a vicar and she worked as a primary-school teacher in one of the local schools. We both became quite close friends as both of us didn't want to be branded with the label of soldier's wife because we had outside interests other than army life. Both of our husbands were going away on the same army manoeuvres for two weeks and Sally asked if I would like to go down to Clacton to stay at her parents' house for a weekend. Sally asked if I minded going to a church service of a different religion from my own. I said no, after all we pray to the same God. So it was settled we would visit Clacton at the weekend. I rang my parents and said I would be away for the weekend and would ring them the moment I returned home. When Sally and I arrived at her parents' home I did not realise it was a country parish rather than being in the centre of a busy location. The church was only across the road from the vicarage and I noticed how old the church really was, dating back to Saxon times. Sally and I settled down to her parents' hospitality and on Saturday we headed to the seaside which was a great feeling of smelling the sea air and enjoying the sea breezes. We decided to have an early night because after the church service we were heading back to Wiltshire. On both nights I slept extremely well. However, early on Sunday morning I was awakened by huge bright blazing sunlight coming through the window which was to the right-hand side of my bed. I noticed a woman standing in the middle of the bright sunshine with golden blonde hair and wearing a long white garment. My first thought was it must be Sally but the light was so strong I must have dozed off back to sleep. I was awakened by a tapping on the door but this time it was Sally who came in to tell me it was time to get up and did I want tea or coffee? I sat up looking very confused and I enquired if Sally had

96

entered the room earlier and she replied no, this was the only time she had come in. I said I must have been dreaming and it had left me feeling woozy. After we had breakfast and went over to the church service, Sally's father said we could climb the church tower to look at the views of the countryside. As I climbed the tower my thoughts were still reeling back to the morning's event of the bright light because I knew that I was wide awake and not sleeping. As we reached the top of the tower I had the feeling of being a soldier on duty looking out over the encampments that once scattered around the church grounds. Was I having one of those experiences of reliving a past life?

I felt really tired and exhausted after the last few days' events and I was so glad to be back at the flat. Before I could really unwind I had to pop out and ring my parents at the local telephone box because we were not connected to the telephone service. I was glad to hear my mother's voice but I noticed a different tone in her voice and then my mother announced that there was some sad family news because my grandfather on my father's side had died. I asked my mother if this had taken place quite early in the morning and she agreed. It was then that I opened up and relayed to my mother what had happened to me. In fact, my mother said, you have been introduced to your guardian angels who informed you that your grandfather had passed over before my own family was delivered of the sad news. Indeed, it was in this flat that my psychic gift was growing from strength to strength by presenting me with situations of people who still lived on the earth plane. For example, my guides would inform me when people would be moving back into the married quarters area. My husband's friend, Keith Saunders, had been posted to Germany but attached to another regiment. I told my husband I had seen Keith walking past the flat and he did not call in. Steve said I must have been mistaken because Keith was still in Germany and it would be another six months before his return. How confusing I thought and then I began to doubt my own sanity. However, the very next day my husband heard that Keith would be part of the early party being sent back to Bulford as the setting up party for his squad and would be living very close to where we live. It was at that flat that I became pregnant and gave birth to a lovely baby boy called Paul. Even during the birth my spirit guides were letting me know that they were working very closely with me by sending me images of comfort from the very saints that I prayed to during my hour of need. Steve and I had a son to look after so we had to decide if we should look to buy a property or stay in married quarters. If we stayed in married quarters until Steve came out of the army the chances were we would be rehoused in a council estate but not in a place of our choice, so we decided to buy our own house and now the property search was on. We did not have long to wait because the local council was working with a group of builders to sell houses purely to first time buyers but you had to meet certain criteria. Luckily we fitted the bill but the only area available was at Swindon because a new town was being created and there were more opportunities for houses to be built. However, Steve would have to move back into single accommodation to finish off his army career and take part in courses to guide him towards a new career path. So I would move into the new house with Paul and Steve would join us six months later.

16

Freshbrook

Swindon is known as the town of roundabouts and there is a particular roundabout that has about six mini-roundabouts coming from one big centred traffic island. Freshbrook is a new large township being created on the outskirts of Swindon located near one of the major highways, the notorious M4 motorway. Most of the new estates had a selection of starter homes which consisted of one- or two-bedroom houses. Steve and I were very excited about buying our first home together. However, we initially saw our home as a sketch at the local council offices and we adored how the properties were portrayed by the artist's impression. So we decided to put a deposit down to secure the property and therefore entered our first mortgage agreement. Also, a decision was made to have a look at the area but we had not expected it to be still an active building site. Once we had driven into the cul-de-sac where our new home was we had to dodge the risen ironworks of unfinished manholes because the roads had not been surfaced. We were very surprised at how many of the properties were already occupied. Our new home was a two-bedroom mid-terrace and there was a total of four properties altogether in a row. No one had moved into our row yet, and it looked like we were going to be the first occupants to move in. The street lights had not been connected so there was a lot of finishing off to do before the estate was completed. After a period of time, came the day for the legal signing of the documents and exchanging of contracts and then we were given a date to finally move into Freshbrook. Once we got the keys for the property this was the first opportunity we had to actually see the inside of our new home. Instantly I was thinking, are we really going to like it? As Steve turned the key in the door he let me be the number one person to enter this small but compact house. My initial impressions were of the smell of fresh paint and how our voices echoed because there was no furniture just an empty shell of a house. From the hallway was a door that brought you into a large living room which also accommodated a single flight of stairs to two bedrooms and a family bathroom. In my mind's eye I could visualise the lounge decorated in what I call earthy colours of creams, browns and terracotta. At the opposite end of the living room was a door into a kitchen-cum-dining room in which I had always wanted a red and white theme and again I could instantly see this image developing before my eyes. Surprisingly, I did end up with all these colours in the various rooms. Just off the dining room was the back door leading out to a long narrow garden that had rows of separate wire fencing to divide the neighbouring gardens. There was a six-foot wooden fence at the bottom of the garden and beyond that was a row of garages. Luckily our garage was just the other side of the wooden fence so Steve had plans to put a garden gate in the fence which was really great in the end. As you ascended the stairs there was a small landing with a doorway leading you to the back bedroom which was the larger of the two bedrooms and this was going to be our bedroom. Back onto the landing was the middle door which was the bathroom. Ironically, this bathroom was the same layout as our previous one in the married quarters. There was no window and the light switch operated the extractor fan, plus the colour green bathroom suite was identical. Finally the last doorway brought you into the front bedroom which was of an odd shape. This was due to accommodating the overhead bulk of the staircase. We decided this would be ideal as our son's bedroom. My overall impression of this property was lovely and then I had a strange feeling wash over me. I knew that this house would only be a stepping stone because my lifestyle would involve looking after my husband and son. I also felt that this was not a home where I could put my roots down. In other words I could not visualise living here for a long period of time. In fact, we only lived in Freshbrook for about a year. Therefore, I knew that I would have no time to fully explore my psychic ability. Maybe spirit decided to conserve my psychic energy for later? Within a few weeks we had organised a rental van and some of Steve's friends offered to help us with the move. Steve got some time off work to help me settle down to my new civilian lifestyle. Once Steve had gone back to barracks I realised I was truly on my own with just a young baby for company. What made matters worse was that the street lighting had still not been connected due to some delay and I was still the only occupier in our terrace. In addition, young Paul suffered from night colic. I felt so alone living in a strange area not knowing anyone and existing under difficult pressures. However, even though I was physically alone I was never spiritually on my own because in my hour of need I always sensed that comfort was close by. Somehow I got into a routine of organising the shopping plus the housework and I decided to try things like making soft furnishings for our new home. To be honest I do not know what I was trying to create or achieve because this house instantly did not feel right. I could not put any real love into making this a perfect home because something was missing. Emotionally I was drained because my feelings towards my husband were changing due to what I can only describe as working with my intuition. Something just did not feel right and it was not post-natal depression. In fact, it was like Steve was safeguarding his intentions from me. Six weeks before Steve finally left the army for good he got accepted as a prison officer which was great. However, the new job involved going to Bristol for about three months to complete a training course. I began to wonder if we would ever be a family unit. I would sit in our bedroom which faced the main road leading into the cul-de-sac and I would know exactly when Steve's car would appear around the corner. Call it a hunch but I would say it was my way of exploring my psychic ability to know when something was going to happen. For example, we got the telephone installed and I would look at the phone knowing that it was going to ring. Plus I could name the person who was on the other end of the line. Freshbrook was a property that certainly opened my eyes for I began to realise just how negative the neighbours were and how sensitive I was to their issues. However, on top of my own problems with Steve this was not ever going to be a happy home. At the end of Steve's training he passed with flying colours and became a prison officer. Therefore he had to pick three locations to see which prison would be allocated to him. In fact, none of Steve's locations was offered to him. Instead he was given a posting at a young offender's institution in the Warwickshire area. This meant we had to search for a new home again. We did have a choice of living in a house owned by the prison service but we decided to buy our next home and keep on the property ladder. Inwardly I knew that our home in Freshbrook was a temporary measure and we would be moving on, but where to? My parents came over from Northern Ireland for a two-week holiday which gave Steve and me the chance of house hunting for our future home. First, we looked at properties in the nearest town to the prison which was Rugby. None of the properties were suitable and we were beginning to feel very downhearted about the whole situation. We were walking through the main shopping arcade to go to the car park area when we noticed a large advertising board for one of the local estate agents. The agents were advertising a property in a village location on a small new housing estate. No sooner did we have the details of the property in our hands we were driving towards the countryside looking for a village called Long Buckby. Once we found the estate and recognised the house with the For Sale sign outside Steve commented that the building of houses was still continuing. We decided to have a closer look and found the show home open. Before we knew it both Steve and I were saying yes to purchase a three-bedroom semi-detached house situated on a corner plot. This time we actually saw that the property only had its foundations built but the builder did guarantee that our house would be given priority. My parents were delighted and went back to Ireland happy because of the outcome. Freshbrook sold quite promptly but the only downside was that the new owners wanted to move in quickly. The only solution was for me to take Paul over to Ireland and stay with my parents and put our furniture into storage. Steve was going to live in the officers' accommodation which he did not mind and it was easy for him to keep popping over to Long Buckby to check on the building progress. After about ten weeks Paul and I were planning our return to our new home in England. Steve had moved in a day before to make sure the furniture arrived on time from being in storage. I often asked myself whether Steve and I were being guided to live in this new village because otherwise we would never have known of its existence. I look back at my home in Freshbrook and with my hand on my heart there were never ever any loving feelings connected to this property. I frequently wondered if it was built on ley lines which can detect positive or negative energy. I recall saying my final goodbyes to the house and closed the front door for the last time. However, I am not a hundred percent sure but I thought I could hear noises coming from within the property. I got into Steve's car and I never looked back at our home in Freshbrook.

17

Spencer Road

Spencer Road is part of a small housing estate called Princess Park because all the roads were commissioned after the Spencer family who have royal connections and are associated with the Northamptonshire area. William Road, Harry Close and Charles Close were just a few names. This undersized complex of family homes was built on the edge of what was regarded as Green Belt. In fact, under no circumstances can anyone build on the land. Spencer Road was just one of many new roads that were being developed in the village of Long Buckby. This was a growing village and could really be called a small town. This old village is actually mentioned in the Domesday Book which means 'Last Judgement'. Steve came to Birmingham airport to pick up me and Paul who was now about eighteen months old. I felt kind of mixed emotions. However, at the back of my mind I had a nagging doubt but I tried to ignore it, putting it down to the anxiety of the journey and settling in a new location. February is not the best month to move into a property because we had no central heating which we planned do later in the spring but as Steve's car entered Spencer Road I spotted our new home and I was filled with excitement. Plus the fact that I was being reunited with our private belongings and furniture. It was hard to believe that I watched this house materialise from just foundations being laid to an actual building. As I entered the building I asked inwardly, 'Dear God please let this property be a nice place to live in.' Once you entered the tiny hallway there were two doors, one on the right which brought you into a galley-type kitchen with a serving hatch to the dining room and a back door that brought you to the back garden area. I was quite happy with the kitchen and decided to dedicate one area as my Irish corner because I had so many little items of value that it would be a shame not to display them. The doorway opposite the kitchen led to the lounge which was a long narrow room with French doors that took you out to the back garden and at the opposite end of the room was a lovely bay window at the front end of the house. The lounge itself was lovely and bright plus I sensed a strong connection to this particular room but I did not know why until much later. Steve and I decided that we would have a red brick fireplace with a chimney breast plus two shelf areas built to house the TV and hi-fi system. In fact, this was completed four months after we moved in. In the lounge there was a secondary door entrance which led to the under-sized dining room with a flight of stairs leading up to the three bedrooms plus a family bathroom. I always felt that the dining room had a dull look to it. Yet, everyone else loved this room. Also, I had a carpenter come in at a later stage plus he blocked in the exposed central heating pipes and put up very decorative wooden shelving for my collection of plates. As you reached the top of the stairs there was a window which faced onto the front of the house. The landing branched off in two different directions. If you turned left there was a bathroom which also housed the hot water tank. This room was very tiny but had a bright outlook due to it facing south. The last door on this side of the landing was our bedroom with a small built-in cupboard plus a recess which I had as a dressing table area. Steve used his DIY skills to make a built-in wardrobe and storage space around the bed area at a later date. This bedroom looked over the back garden area. Finally, approaching the landing on the right hand side brought you to a small box bedroom which was to be Paul's room. The third bedroom was just a mirror image of our bedroom but Steve built a single wardrobe in the recess because there were no real storage areas in this property. We began to settle down as a family and acquire a daily routine. For example, Steve would go to work at the local prison which was about ten miles away and I would attend mums and tots or the resident playgroup with Paul. I found out that attending these types of event helps you to make new friends plus I was beginning to feel really happy. Also, I had started making soft furnishings for our new home and if truth be told putting my energy into making the situation work. However, peace and harmony was shattered in the form of a telephone call totally out of the blue from Steve's friend Keith who had been once more attached from his regiment and returned to the UK to join his unit in Warminster plus there was talk of a reunion of all the lads getting together. Keith invited Steve and me plus Paul to stay for the weekend with his wife Olga who was German and their children because they had four-bedroomed married quarters. Steve had known Keith and Olga long before they got married. In fact, it was Steve that brought them together because they had a huge row which could have separated them for good. I had the weirdest sensation about this forthcoming journey that it must not take place. Why should something try to warn me about an innocent reunion between old friends? I never told Steve how I felt about the situation or maybe he would not understand. Paul was about three years old and I had never left him in the care of a babysitter and if we went on this journey Keith's baby minder would also look after Paul. Eventually, the day came and I was just not myself. I cannot describe how I felt about what lay ahead of me. I was not excited about Steve meeting an old friend. Halfway into the journey our car, which was getting pretty old, decided to spring a leak in the radiator. I immediately thought, great, we can return home, but no was the reply because Steve always carried bits and pieces to do with the car and he found a solution to pour into the radiator. This meant our journey was back on but I believe it was a spiritual sign to say return home or face what is in front of you. The event that took place on this particular weekend scarred our marriage for life because unknown to me Steve and Olga had some sort of deep feelings towards each other. During our stay I had the unfortunate experience of walking in and finding my husband in bed with Olga. I suddenly realised all the signs were there; why oh why had I not stood my ground and insisted on our return journey home? However, the journey back home was in complete silence; neither of us spoke. Yet, I was mentally chatting to my spirit guides telling them of my future plans that one day I would walk away from my husband and never return to him. I felt very determined that once I left Spencer Road I would certainly make a point of returning only to pick up my personal belongings. In fact, I did keep my promise as you will read later. Life in Spencer Road began to take on a new dimension because I began to recognise the signs of when my angels were around me. I became stressed out due to the fact that Steve began to play mental mind games by packing his bags saying he was leaving us and this would happen around the early hours of the morning. I would be crying then our son would be really upset. Steve would bang the front door loudly and unexplained noises would come from anything electrical within the house even though they were not plugged in. I believe that my angels were letting me know that every time I called out for help it was a symbol to say, we are listening and you are not alone. However, Steve's walking out never lasted more than about six to eight hours then he would waltz back in as if nothing happened but something did take place; I know I had become a stronger person. The situation between Steve and I was getting most unpleasant and yet when I saw family or friends I tried to carry on as if nothing was wrong. As each day went by I became more aware of strange happenings around me because at evening time I liked to sit in the lounge on my own when Paul and Steve had gone to bed. I began to notice how the lounge would glow a warm golden colour as if someone had switched on a bright yellow light. When this occurred the room felt very silent and peaceful plus I felt very relaxed. This happened many times. In fact, I recall an even stranger turn of events in the dining room. Here our telephone was installed so you would not be disturbed by the television. However, during one occasion on an evening when I went to answer the telephone I happened to glance at my reflection in the window when I suddenly caught sight of myself. I was shocked to see a blue-yellow flame rising from the top of my head. I instantly thought about Jesus and his apostles and how they were portrayed with little flames protruding from their heads to represent a sign that the Holy Ghost is within them. Was this my Holy Ghost I often wondered?

My son Paul was showing the early signs of becoming psychic because he began to talk about his imaginary friend Big Bear. However, Big Bear I believe came into Paul's life to guide him because it was around the same time that Steve and I seemed to do nothing but argue. Even Paul's school friends would ask who Big Bear was. Even if I tried to explain to them would they have understood? As Paul was getting older I decided to look for work but the hours would have to be flexible due to the school holidays. The following day I put an advert in the local newsagent for anyone requiring a cleaner/housekeeper. I was quite surprised at the response and not long after I had enough work to earn a decent wage. As the enquiries kept flooding in I had this idea of setting up a cleaning business which I named Pollyanna's because when I called home my father would always say, 'It's Pollyanna from over the sea.' My cleaning business grew and at one point I employed about fifteen women. I was very happy because I enjoyed my new role and it helped me to take my mind off my domestic problems with Steve. I don't think Steve liked the idea of me gaining independence. Strange events happened when I would be cleaning certain houses, such as seeing and sensing spirit energies of past tenants who still roamed their beloved homes. It was through Pollyanna's cleaning business that I met a very talented clairvoyant/medium called Barbara Ford. Barbara had moved into Long Buckby and was seeking part-time employment and had seen my advert looking for cleaning staff. One night Barbara came round to my home for drinks and a chat and before I knew it she was telling me all sorts of information related to myself plus my family. Apparently, this type of psychic enlightenment is called a reading. I was really amazed at what Barbara said but even more astonished when she announced I was psychic too and could do the same type of work. Barbara had taken me under her wing and passed her knowledge on to me for which I shall always be very grateful. When Barbara and I were together unexplained things would happen. For example, Barbara was getting remarried and she invited me to their wedding reception which was being held in an old building that dated back to the late eighteenth century. Therefore, one would expect spirits who had passed over to be very active. In fact, they were because I noticed every time Barbara walked among her wedding guests she kept making the gesture of brushing off imaginary items on her shoulders. In addition, I detected images of smoke rising up from the ground. I looked around the room to see if anyone else had seen what had taken place but the guests were enjoying themselves chatting to each other. I could no longer think straight; I needed to know some answers and who better to ask but Barbara? Indeed, Barbara acknowledged she did have some spiritual energy trying to tune into her psychic abilities of communing with the spirit world hence her actions of pushing them away. I told her about the smoke images which she claimed to be plasma associated with spiritual energy trying to become full-blown spiritual sightings. I really did benefit from Barbara's extra spiritual knowledge because I was able to allow myself to build upon this strong foundation to assist me on my spiritual journey. When I look back to the time just before my mother passed away, once more a strange event happened when all our family received a phone call from our mother wishing us all a happy new year, but on the twenty-eighth of December. I replied to my mother, surely I will be talking to you before New Year's Eve? On New Year's Eve I received a frantic phone call from my sister saying our mother had been rushed into hospital and it did not look too good and was there was a possibility of getting a flight across to Belfast. Had my mother foreseen her time on the earth plane was coming to an end? I told Steve and he was not overly bothered but at the same time never offered to accompany me on this difficult journey so I just went ahead frightened of what I would hear when I reached the other side of the Irish Sea. Unfortunately my mother was truly on her way of passing over between the two worlds when I arrived at the hospital. It was a sad occasion for all the family because our mother always wanted to have her family altogether and even on her deathbed that was not to be for Eileen my older sister was seriously ill and was under doctor's orders not to fly or even attempt to make the journey. Later that evening we received a phone call from the undertaker informing us that our mother's corpse was being released from the morgue. This caused great panic as it was all hands on deck trying to sort out which room we should use for our mother to lay to rest. I walked into my parents' sitting room and the vision before my eyes was the silk flowers that would normally be placed in the silver rose bowl scattered all over the floor. There was no explanation for this weird happening because there were no young babies in our family at that

111

time. As I picked up the flowers I noticed there were four of the same colour and one of a different colour. Was this a sign from our mother to express her love for her four daughters and one son? Armed with this information about being able to communicate with both the living and the spirits I was feeling exhilarated.

I required my independence because Steve told me once I was never to ask how much he earned, it was his money not mine so I never knew how much he earned, so what else could I do but take on any type of extra employment that would allow me to earn extra money for Paul and myself? Fortunately I was able earn extra money by waitressing in an up and coming restaurant in a neighbouring village. During my employment I was quite happy because it was spiritually active. For example, the restaurant was originally a purpose-built stable and everywhere I went I felt the presence of a man who was still looking after his horses. Eventually, the staff and owners became aware of this special gift, that I was born with giving snippets of information of past, present and future events. My employers would often ask if I would entertain the clients with my party piece as we nicknamed it. In fact, the clients could not get enough of it because they were fascinated about how accurate the information was. One Saturday evening the assistant manager Philip asked if I could see him in his office. All sorts of things were running through my mind. Had a customer complained, etc? In fact, Philip had been headhunting me to join an elite group of waiters and waitresses to work under his watchful eye for one of the highest society families in Northamptonshire. Unknown to me Philip had worked for this particular family a long time ago as a butler but a death occurred in this family which meant that the only son would be taking over as head of the household and all the duties connected with the estate. Therefore, the young earl was reorganising the household staff and Philip was asked to be the head butler. Also, he was asked to deal with bringing in casual waiting staff for both family and corporate catering events. Philip was a perfectionist and this is why he wanted people he could rely upon. It is really uncanny how situations come about. For example, when Steve and I went shopping in Northampton we would have to pass Althorp House, the family home of the Spencer Family. However, I always felt a longing or knowing sensation that some day I would actually drive beyond the big iron gates and not just drive past. After accepting this wonderful opportunity I could not wait to start work at the big house. I was very nervous about mixing with the gentry and trying to remember to watch my mannerisms at all times. I recall the very first time I entered Althorp House all the catering staff had strict instructions to arrive at the tradesman's entrance. I remember ringing the doorbell and when the door opened there was a hive of activity going on with staff dashing off in different directions but the aroma of food cooking was very welcoming. I really enjoyed working at the big house because it took my mind off Steve and our issues. About six months after I started working at Althorp unknown to me my name was put forward for the position of weekend housekeeper. This was due to the fact that I had cleaning experience and I ran my own domestic cleaning business. After being interviewed by the young earl and his wife they decided to offer me the position which I accepted. In fact, I stayed for two years employed as weekend housekeeper to the Spencer family. The role involved having access to both private and public areas of this lovely stately home. This property was like my main training ground before I graduated as a clairvoyant/medium. For example, I can remember walking behind one of the waitresses as she was carrying a huge tray but when I looked at her I saw a smoky outline of a female dressed in clothing from the Tudor period. Another strange occurrence was in one of the many sitting rooms I was at my station waiting for the young earl and his guests to arrive when a voice or thought from nowhere said take note of the white sculptured ornaments on the fireplace because they are made locally. I soon forgot all about the incident and only remembered when I was chatting to Philip the butler and asked him if he knew anything about the creator of such items. What a picture my face must have been when he replied that they were created by a local sculptor many centuries ago. Was an unknown energy trying to test me or teach me about my psychic skills?

Entering certain rooms I would feel both hot and cold areas where spiritual energy had been. I enjoyed the history of the house and the interesting people that would come and go from the property. People and various situations in general would be presented to me in my life-path as if I was being tested on all levels of both physical and mental emotions to see if I was a fit pupil to become a person who can connect to the spirit world. I remember a staff trip was being organised through Althorp House to Canterbury for the day. I had never been to Canterbury before so I asked Steve if we could take Paul and for once he agreed. Just as we disembarked the coach and headed towards the town centre there was a complete power cut all over the town. I thought, wait a minute what are these signs trying to say? Strangely enough we ended up going to the huge cathedral which was not affected by the power cut and by visiting this place of worship I spotted a tiny little shop that had customers still coming and going from the premises. The shop was like a little emporium selling an array of spiritual goods including tarot cards which I was drawn towards so in the end I purchased a set. However, I was never able to bring myself to use the cards because the timing was not right or I was not meant to meddle with the cards just yet. In fact, it was about eight years later before I felt really comfortable about using the tarot cards and I have never looked back.

Since working at Althorp House I decided to go into adult

114

education and I was lucky to get a place at the local college for four and a half days on what was called an access course covering various subjects such as maths, English, etc. At this point of my life I really sensed the need to study because when I was younger I always had the impression that I would be holding back the class if I asked questions. In fact, I just sat at the back of the class and pretended to understand what the lesson was all about. During the course all access students had a week off to do something connected to a subject they were studying for. The student had to raise money to pay or support themselves in the venture of their own choice. My friend Amy and myself chose to go to Dublin because we were studying James Joyce. Our English tutor who was also from an Irish background decided to come along as well. Amy and I stayed in a hotel in the Temple Bar district of Dublin while our tutor and her friend stayed in a different location. I remembered when the aeroplane landed at Dublin airport once the aeroplane doors were opened and I stepped onto Dublin ground I had this huge overwhelming emotion as if I had been there before but I had not; this was my first trip to Dublin. Our chosen hotel was originally a converted bank and from the moment of our arrival I knew exactly which window would be our bedroom. Once again it was as if I had gained inside information because we were directed to the room that was three floors up with the window on the corner of the building overlooking a very narrow side street. On the first night we both felt very tired and excited about our visit to Dublin so we decide to have an early night. I remember Amy chatting to me and the next thing I could hear in the background was the lonely sound of the tin whistle being played by a young street urchin boy. However, then I heard the sound of horses hooves trotting on the cobblestones followed by a lot of activity. Eventually when I fully awakened I asked Amy if she had slept well and she said yes, but she commented that while she was chatting to me I had fallen into a deep sleep. Amy was amazed when I told her of the sounds that I had heard. How did I know it was a boy playing the instrument and the horses belonged to the travelling people? Once again spirit energies had tuned into my waveband which I was beginning to find enchanting.

It was not long after my trip to Dublin that I had to prepare for my exams in June. I asked my angels and spirit guides to assist me in my hour of need. As a result, I got an overall seventy-eight per cent which was equal to two A-level passes; enough to be accepted at a university. Plus I sat an extra exam, the RSA stage 1 in numeracy and I got a credit much to my surprise. I applied to Nene College which now has been granted university status. Steve was not overly impressed that I had succeeded in getting this far but I was really pleased with myself. Going to university meant spending more money on petrol and the books that were required for the various studies. I remember a weird incident when I walked past a tutor who was head of the English department and he turned around and commented to me, 'You have a very strong aura around you and people know when you walk into an area.' Up to that point I had never ever spoken to that person before or after that particular conversation. To me that was a very strange exchange yet people today do say that I walk with an air of authority even though I am only four foot eight inches tall. I had just completed a month into my second year at university and I was struggling to pay for the various textbooks. One evening my friend Lisa invited me up to the social club and this became a regular once a week visit. I enjoyed the chance of meeting different people and relaxing in a warm atmosphere. On one of these occasions the landlord of the club asked Lisa if she would like some casual bar work but she declined and instead asked if I would like to accept the offer. Well, it is strange because I had worked in the kitchen helping to prepare meals and other various jobs many months before but I had never seen myself working behind the bar. Also, I asked myself why I had come full circle working in the social club for a second time but there must be a reason as you will find out soon. During the month of November the social club decided to run an event to raise money for the under-eleven football team. As it was a charity event the women had to dress up as the male footballers and the men dressed up as the women. This event took place on a Sunday afternoon and we actually had the first snow of winter. Prior to the start of the match I had to go up to the social club and help the men with their outfits and make-up. There was one bloke who had some kind of an effect on me and I had to speak to him so I commented on his outfit. At that point I did not know his name or even if he was married. Believe it or not fate had held in reserve bringing us together and during one of our conversations we found out I had actually served him at the posh restaurant where I had previously worked. Somebody upstairs, as I nicknamed the spirit world, wanted to bring us together. This gentleman's name was Howard Morgan. Howard and I gelled from day one because I knew from the moment I met him I had found my soulmate. This was not a teenage crush, but I had never felt like this before about any man. Even though Howard is five years younger than I age means nothing to two people who really understand each other. We met in November 1997 and I moved in with Howard in January 1998 to stay at his mum's house. My son Paul decided he would like to stay with his father but we would see each other on a regular basis plus staying over once we found a place to rent. A new life-path was quickly evolving around me and I was very contented plus excited because at last I was at peace not only with myself but with who I really am: a natural clairvoyant/ medium. I knew then that I had to move forward if I was to succeed with the lifestyle that spirit was setting out in front of me. I was sad and upset about leaving my son temporarily but never heartbroken about leaving Spencer Road.

18

School Cottage

When I left Spencer Road, Howard had previously moved back into his mother's property because his marriage had broken down due to his wife having an affair. Howard's mum's house was to become my temporary home until we got a rented place. Howard's mum's house was situated in an area called Watford Village about three miles from Long Buckby. This village used to have a large manor house which dominated the area in past times when gentry ruled the outlying district. The land belonged to the Henley family of Watford parish, who also owned most of the parish. In 1975 Lord Henley died unexpectedly and without taking precautions to protect his estate from death duties. So heavy taxes destroyed the Henley estate. Therefore, most of the estate was being sold off including Watford Court, a huge and imposing manor house. Within two years this house of some architectural repute had been demolished to make way for executive homes. Watford village is not far from the A5, a major road but otherwise known as Watling Street, a reminder of the Roman method of road building dominating a natural pass into the Midlands area. Even now, Howard's mum rents one of the many properties still owned by the Henley estate. Howard had previously heard that one of the properties opposite his mum's house was coming up for rent. With great enthusiasm we got the keys to look at the property. What a nightmare because the house was mid-terrace and had only one main door entrance which served as front and back door. This property could only be approached by crossing over either side of your neighbour's back garden which could be terrible if you did not get on with the neighbours. Howard and I viewed the house but each room we entered our hearts sank lower and lower because the property required so much work to make it habitable. Also, there was the problem of keeping such a house warm because it only had one fireplace and that was in the lounge. Therefore, this particular property was a no go situation. We handed the keys back to the village postmistress whose property was also owned by the Henley estate. She dealt with handling the keys of rented properties so people would make an appointment and she would give the key to them to view the property. However, she did mention another property was coming up for rent, again it was opposite Howard's mum's house. Was this an omen that we should live in Watford village? Furthermore, I had been told of this individual property by my clairvoyant friend Barbara. In fact, the way Barbara described it for me was, 'You will have a peek into your future.' I did not know exactly what she meant until one day when I was still living at Long Buckby with Steve I was driving through the village of Watford and noticed a For Rent sign outside a beautiful old stone cottage set back from the main busy road. I stopped my car and actually went up to the property and looked through the windows. Indeed, I knew one day I would be living there and that it would only be a matter of time which came in the form of my long-term marriage break up and moving into this property with my boyfriend Howard who eventually became my husband. Howard's mum rang him at work with good news saying we could collect the keys for School Cottage as a viewing had been arranged for us. We were both very excited at the news of possibly settling down in our own home soon. School Cottage is a lovely old property that dates back to 1856. It had three eaves protruding at the front and two downstairs windows plus an extra large front door. Yet there were no windows to the back of the house because it was classed as a three-quarter type property where everything happens at the front. A hideous lean-to extension was added at a later date built in modern red brick. School Cottage would have been purposely built for the headmaster and his family plus it belonged to the Henley estate. Also, attached to School Cottage was a very derelict schoolroom that was in addition used as a village hall before the local residents got together and built a big village hall. As Howard and I approached the shared driveway of School Cottage I knew this was going to be our home even though we did not have any household items between us, only love for each other. Yet, people from what I would call the old school rallied around getting us items to furnish our future home. We could not use the front door because no one had opened it for years. Everything was in its natural state except for the modern plumbing, fireplaces and the hideous extension. This house had the original door latches and stone window frames with the unique glass that was so thin, not like the glass you find in our homes today, plus the window ledges were so wide. Therefore, School Cottage was full of character features. As we entered the back door which was located on the front side of the house there in front of us was a sloping floor going uphill and a door off to the right-hand side which was the compact bathroom. As you approached the very tiny kitchen a huge wall-mounted water tank on one wall only left room for the cooker, fridge, washing machine and the all-important sink. The kitchen was so small that with two people in it it was crowded. From the kitchen was a door that brought you into what we called a dining room but in actual fact it would have been used as a kitchen/dining room and most likely housed an inglenook fireplace. Over in the far right-hand corner of the room was a door recess which led into the old schoolroom but had been blocked up for

121

many years. As I stood by the kitchen/dining room threshold I could see a lady, very petite with her hair pinned up in a bun. She was wearing a long dress and had an apron folded up towards her and was feeding chickens. I could see her but could she me? Straightaway I told Howard and he said, 'I'm not living anywhere that has ghosts.' My reply was, 'It is the living you have to fear not the dead.' After my brief introduction with our first spiritual energy Howard waited for me as we viewed the rest of the house together. From the dining room was a door that brought you into a big wide hallway which had a flight of stairs that had a small landing and then you had to turn left up a second flight of stairs which had a small wide landing plus a window and two bedroom doors opposite each other. There were two other doors leading off the downstairs hallway. One door entrance was very narrow and this door was situated under the stairwell which we were to use as a storage area. Yet, it was fascinating how this house was built because inside the understair storage area we could see actual earth and no damp-proof course as you would find in modern houses of today. Finally, the last door brought you into a warm, bright room but not very large in size. It had a lovely tiled fireplace but sadly the majority of the tile features were either cracked or had pieces broken off. Once you climbed up the two flights of stairs the top landing appeared to be wider than a normal house which was great for us because the house was lacking storage space. The first door to the right brought you into a lovely big square bedroom with a chimney breast at one end of the room and of course a window facing onto the front. I personally fell in love with this room. Did something here want us to move in here with them? What a different feeling when you entered the second front bedroom. It was immediately freezing in here and looked completely dull and lifeless. Yet, these two bedrooms were mirror images of each other except the ceiling was about to fall down but this was repaired at a later date. It was time to go outside and see what other delights were in store for us. Attached to the property was quite a big area of land which was used for allotments to help feed the tenants of the estate-owned properties. We planned to keep cutting the overgrown grass until it looked like a decent lawn. Also, there were three sheds dotted around, two for storage and one for coal plus a concrete area, which was to become dog kennels at a later date, and a small rockery area. You had full view of the old schoolroom because the windows were on our side of the property so I could not resist just looking through and what a shock! There before my eyes was a little red-haired boy but it looked like he had a problem with his legs because he walked with the aid of crutches. Again this was spirit energies coming forward letting me see them, but why? The old schoolroom looked like it was in a time capsule because you had the old measuring stick still fixed to the wall for measuring the children's height. After viewing the complete house we entered the living room and it felt like the room was crowded with spiritual energy awaiting our decision to see if we were going to rent this property. Howard and I looked at each other and we both agreed that we should take on the rental of this wonderful old house and all its spiritual inhabitants. Howard being very practical also pointed out that this house did not come with any luxuries like central heating and we would have to depend on the coal fires plus storage heaters to keep us warm in future winters. As we walked back down the driveway after locking our new home up nice and securely I was not absolutely sure if I had seen the image of an old woman looking out of the second bedroom window; I said to Howard, 'Our house is in the safe hands of Mrs Feldman' and that was when we nicknamed our ghostly lodger.

Within a period of four weeks School Cottage was signed over to our care and boy, what special attention did we give it. We moved in straightaway and it was really surprising how much furniture we had collected or acquired. For example, most of our potential furniture came from people who had passed over. School Cottage made me feel much more secure or maybe it was because I was truly happy for the first time in my life. We decided to paint and decorate where and when extra money became available. At a later time we put a gas fire in and built a stone fire surround in our lounge which made a big difference to our home comforts. However, I was in my second year at university and I decided to put studying aside because it was hard for Howard to keep the both of us on one wage. To earn money I went back into house cleaning but this time I kept to about six properties and this brought in sufficient for us to have holidays plus purchase items for our home. Howard and I felt a special bonding towards School Cottage because we felt that we just wanted to try and preserve something that was as loving and beautiful as this old house.

The gardening jobs would be shared between Howard and me. For example, Howard would cut the grass and I would cut the hedge, prune and do the weeding. It was not long before we both agreed it would be nice to have a dog and we ended up with Bob, a Scottish Border Collie, followed by Pennie, a Heinz variety, and Sprocket the black cat. Our first Christmas was very special because we both went out and chose a real Christmas tree and bought all the decorations. Howard decided to place the tree inside a box to hide the fact it would be standing in a bucket of water so that the tree did not dry out. While Howard was using an electric jigsaw he noticed that every time he put it down the saw would start up on its own. Howard called me to come and witness the event. Even when Howard switched off the electricity the saw would still switch itself on somehow. I decided to experiment and started speaking to the saw and sure enough it was as if something was using the saw as a form of communicating.

Another incident happened around Howard as he was working in the hallway when he suddenly saw a woman who I had described earlier with her hair up in a bun wearing clothes not of our period but she just disappeared into where the family pet dog was lying. This had shaken Howard. Up to that point he was a non-believer but now his views were changing. Since that occurrence lots of strange things began to happen. Quite often when we were sitting in the living room you could hear soft footsteps climbing the stairs plus someone walking across our bedroom floor but yet we knew that we where the only people in the house.

One of my friends asked if we had room for two fireside chairs which we accepted because the previous owner had passed away. When we brought the chairs home we were trying to decide where they would fit in. Howard suddenly made a screaming noise and jumped to one side. I asked what the problem was and he said it felt like someone or thing was poking him in the back plus it was coming from the direction of where the chairs were standing. Bob our dog instantly sat up and started barking towards the chair.

One night I was either woken up or I naturally sensed another person in the room standing at the bottom of our bed. I was not frightened but intrigued by it all. Another evening not long after we had both retired to bed Howard sat up quickly because he thought someone was outside shining a torch up at the bedroom windows. He got up and looked out the window but there was no one there and no vehicles had gone past. According, to Howard's mum strange lights had been seen frequently around this area and some said UFO sightings have been active. While I have lived in this property I have never felt frightened even when Howard was working on his night shift. I sensed that my strength and wisdom grew within me more. I felt I had to live in this property because it always presented me with more psychic knowledge than anyone could imagine. For example, my husband used to participate in motor-cross racing, a sport he really enjoyed doing. Howard's aunt and uncle would accompany us because his uncle would ride in competition as well. It was on one of the weekend events held near Canada Heights down in the Kent area that I was introduced to the fairies. We arrived at the racetrack about 5.30 p.m. on the Friday evening. Everyone felt tired as we battled our way through the start of the weekend traffic. As we drove around the site looking for somewhere to make camp an area was located. This particular area had tall trees mixed with hedgerows and shrubs in a pretty sheltered place. Howard and his uncle got out of their transit vans to survey the area while I sat in the van just gazing out of the window at this barrier of greenery in front of me. All of a sudden a huge breeze from nowhere began to shake the trees and shrubs and before my eyes about a dozen fairies appeared. The fairies were about eighteen inches tall and had beautiful semi-transparent wings that seemed to project colour. However, they began to make gestures of 'go back' with their hands. I realised they were asking us not to park near the hedgerow but to move elsewhere. I could not believe what I had seen. I called Howard over to the van and asked if we would be better off parking near the road as it would make it easier for our departure on Sunday. So camp was set up in a different location. All evening I could not get settle down just thinking back to the earlier events of the day. No one would believe me if I told them. On Saturday we went for a drive out to see a bit more of the region. We arrived at a place called Southend-on-Sea which had a long pier over the sea so we decided walk along it because there were some little shops, etc. However, we were surprised to see the pirate radio ship Radio Caroline docked alongside the pier. As we were making our way back I noticed a garden shed but it was being used by a clairvoyant who had pictures of Des O'Connor who she had previously read for. Therefore, I thought if it is good enough for Des

126

then it is good enough for me so I went and was very surprised by what she had to say. The reading consisted of my getting married but at that time Howard and I had not even been engaged. However, that Christmas Howard bought me a beautiful single diamond engagement ring. While we were away from the race track a group of our friends had arrived and set up camp exactly where the fairies had previously warned us off. Also, there had been a charity mountain bike ride on the actual track which our friends had taken part in. However, just as we arrived back from our outing Gill, one of the guys' wife, was running towards us in hysterics shouting something about her husband Bob. Bob had taken part in the charity race but hit a boulder that threw him off his bike and he ended up breaking his wrist in the most horrific manner which required pinning. Everyone was shocked by the accident but I felt a million questions running through my mind. Such as, was the fairies' warning just for us or was I supposed to move everybody away from that cursed piece of ground? On the Sunday I could not muster up the energy to leave our caravan to watch Howard race.

Eventually when I did emerge out of the caravan I suddenly realised Howard's aunt and uncle plus our caravan had been parked either side of a huge oak tree which represents the tree of life. So really the fairies showed themselves as protectors, warning me of a *future* event. It was only after Bob's accident that I actually told Howard and his aunt and uncle because I thought they would laugh but they did not. I realised instantly how people do believe in the power of fairies.

After my brief encounter with the little folk life began to settle down for a short period before I had another weird experience. Again we were heading up to another motor-cross scramble in Cumbria to spend the weekend with our friends. It was the thirty-first of August 1997. Howard was driving and he reminded me we were not far from the race

127

track location when suddenly I had a vision of Princess Diana and her friend Dodi Al Fayed. I questioned myself, why was I being shown a vision of these two very important people, but in my vision they looked very happy smiling and laughing together. As we drove into the location of where the racing competition was going to be held there was no time for hanging around, everyone wanted to head off to the pub. The following morning you could hear all sorts of noises coming from the vans and tents that appeared to be scattered everywhere, not forgetting the smell of fried breakfast wafting through the encampment. Howard had woken up and turned his radio on because he wanted to hear what the weather forecast was going to be for racing conditions when instantly the radio announced that Princess Diana and her companion Dodi Al Fayed had been involved in a car accident in Paris. Soon the horrible news had spread like wildfire around the encampment. Grown men had tears in their eyes and the women found it hard to accept the fact that such a caring lovely lady should be taken from us just when she had found her own happiness. Everyone was subdued for the rest of the day. However, somehow I knew a piece of jewellery was to be found in the car and I nearly fainted when the news reporter said on the evening news that a ring was found in the car. On the day of Princess Diana's funeral strange occurrences started to happen around our home. At the same time as the late Princess was approaching Althorp House I was repairing a tent that our dog had damaged. Howard was watching television in our bedroom and I was dashing between the two bedrooms where I had set up the sewing machine. The sewing machine started to sew without the aid of anyone pushing on the foot treadle. We both looked at each other and then ran into the second bedroom but believe it or not I had to prise the treadle apart and pull the lead from the machine but it still worked even without power. The amazing thing was that the sewing cotton was not even knotted up.

Neither of us could explain what had just taken place in School Cottage.

Why all of a sudden should I get weird feelings about people's health I asked myself, because I began to sense something was not right when I spoke to my father in Ireland on the telephone. My father's voice sounded like something had robbed him of his inner energy. Maybe I had sensed it more because of living away from my family but I did pass on my fears to my sisters that our father did not sound a well man. After a short period of time I received a telephone call saying he had had a slight stroke but a much larger one had overcome him and he was in the intensive care unit. Arrangements were made for Howard and me to fly over to Belfast. It was really strange having to pack clothes in case a funeral took place but in this case it actually happened. We arrived at the hospital. Only close family was allowed in to see my father. Strange, but this was the first time any of my family had ever met Howard. As I entered the intensive care unit I was prepared to see my father with tubes and machines surrounding him but it was still a shock because he looked so frail just lying there. Instantly I took my father's right hand and spoke to him, telling I had just arrived from England. Even though his eyes was closed his fingers traced the outline of the rings that I was wearing and then his hand went limp. I knew that was my father's way of saying, 'Its okay, you're here, that is all that matters.' I joined the remaining family members plus Howard in a room that was set aside for events like this where family and friends can be together when a loved one is going through the dying process. Each and every one of us was supporting each other which did help the situation. We got news that our father had been moved to a corner position of the ward where he could pass away peacefully with his family. Howard's purpose was to assist me in this difficult time of need and he also wanted to ask my father for his daughter's hand in marriage which he did do. My family was so pleased for me and it lightened the atmosphere in our difficult times. We stayed with my father till we knew he had passed over and we evoked the assistance of my mother and my father's parents, all of whom had passed over to see our father through his transition to a spiritual world.

On returning home to School Cottage I seemed to be able to link into the spirit world more freely. It was as if a huge cover had been removed from me. The strange thing was people started to ring up for readings and parties. All of this was new to me but Howard always encouraged me to go forward especially with my psychic ability. Another weird occurrence was Howard asked me to marry him on the fourth of December which only allowed me about ten weeks to get everything organised. When I look back, the number four is a number that has followed me through my life-path. For example, I was born in the fourth month, April, thirteen was the date which comes to four when you add the two numbers together, I am the fourth daughter and I got married on the fourth and the list goes on. After my father's death I began to get a bit unsettled about my cleaning jobs and a neighbour asked if I would consider doing some office work in a warehouse in Daventry. I could not believe it and jumped at the chance. Not long after I started working in the office I recall a memory of a strange dream. I can remember seeing a house and as I was standing straight in front of the house I knew there would be a door of to the left. Also, I knew it had a water connection to the right-hand side of the building. I never knew where this house was nor did I see any other rooms.

My previous husband Steve had decided to sell Spencer Road and once the money side of things was sorted out Howard and I would start looking at houses. It was very weird because Howard and I used to drive around a new residential housing estate but Howard said that such places were built like rabbit warrens. We stopped in a cul-de-sac and before either of us got out of the car Howard said, 'Look at that house with the sloping driveway, that would be no good for us.' In fact, one weekend we had just viewed an ex-council house in one of the local villages but it had a very depressing vibes and Howard suggested we should look at the new houses in Daventry. The sales negotiator said she had two houses side by side available but the end terrace would suit our requirements and gave us the key and directions to where the house was. I had to laugh because it was the one with the sloping driveway. Once I turned the key in the door and opened the door I knew I had seen the layout of this house before. Actually this was the house I had foreseen because the canal is only a ten-minute walk to the right-hand side of the house. Both of us fell in love with this property so we immediately paid a deposit and within six weeks we had exchanged the contracts. It was very sad packing up and leaving School Cottage because it was our first home together and we had very fond memories of this property. School Cottage was very much portrayed as my secret agent assisting me with the last few spiritual lessons before I was sent on my way in the world full of sceptics. However, I often think about our spiritual friend Mrs Feldman, was she still there?

19

29 Harrow Lane

Daventry was originally known as Daintree and dates back to early Roman times. Nowadays it is a busy market town which lies near the Grand Union Canal. Northampton is only thirteen miles away and London is a further seventy miles. Daventry is a very historic town known for manufacturing whips and shoes. In the old coaching days it was a great throughfare to the North West part of England. Daventry is still growing, not only in size but also in population. As a result, huge areas of farmland have been sold off to accommodate new housing complexes, schools and shopping centres. Harrow Lane is part of a small housing estate with a total of eighty houses, both two to three bedroom properties. This estate is situated on the edge of the complex boundary. In fact, one would say we have the best of both worlds because we have the town centre about half an hour walking distance and the countryside an instant five minute walk away in the opposite direction. The houses on this new estate all appear to be different because each new householder is trying to outshine their neighbours by becoming very individual with their tastes in gardens plus how to dress their windows. Howard and I both agreed from the very first time we viewed this property something was drawing us towards the house and we had to purchase it. The small hallway had a flight of stairs and to the left was the lounge. I found this room to have a divine and relaxing feeling even though it had no carpets; it was just painted in magnolia which was a standard colour for the interior of new properties. There was a pair of glass double doors leading into the kitchen/diner. The moment I approached this room that was it for me because I instantly knew this would be our new home. The kitchen was fitted in light beech-coloured units plus pretty biscuit-coloured tiles that almost looked like they had been individually hand-crafted with the odd white tile for contrast. From the dining room was a pair of patio doors leading onto a small paved patio plus a turf lawn. This particular garden was the same size as the three-bedroom houses because it was an end of terrace. At the top of the stairs was a small landing which had three doors. The first door led to the bathroom which was situated at the rear of the property. This was a very compact room but we had a choice of a bath or shower which was not offered at the old house. The middle door was the back bedroom, of an average size. You could put a double or two single beds in this room. The last room was the front bedroom or master bedroom. This room looked like a cottage room because the window was designed to be part of an eave. The ceiling sloped to one side with two alcoves. When I stood in this room which had a very bright appearance I could actually visualise our bedroom furniture there.

Howard and I staggered our move into the new house because we kept the rented property for an extra month. By planning the move this way we were able to bring boxes of items over after we finished work. On one occasion Howard had left the new house and had gone back to School Cottage to start preparing the dinner while I stayed to finish off sewing hems on the new lounge curtains. Howard rang my mobile to see if I was ready to come home and I replied it would take about thirty minutes to complete the job. I was so busy concentrating on finishing the curtain hems when I sensed the feeling that I was not alone. I suddenly looked to my right and sensed the energy of a gentleman from the spirit world. Also I noticed he was wearing a pair of grey-coloured trousers which my father would have worn when he was alive on the earth plane. In fact, I did not feel panic or fear, actually it was a heartfelt experience knowing that my father approved of our new home and was still looking after my well-being.

I decided to give our house a name. I took both my parents' Christian names and came up with the title of Kathbern House in their loving memory. This house is a very special property because I class it as being an extremely lucky house where money is concerned. Prior to us buying the house we had filled in some forms at the show home when we had previously visited. In the meantime we put the deposit down to secure the property. Then we received information from the house builders making us a money offer should we purchase one of their homes. Normally, Howard would throw away anything to do with advertising but his intuition was telling him to chase this situation up by making a telephone call. The outcome was the building company apologised and offered us a further two thousand pounds off the asking price of the property. Furthermore, not long after we had moved into Harrow Lane I joined the office Lottery syndicate for just fifty pence per week. I had only been in the group for about four weeks when we had a huge win of about two hundred and eighty thousand pounds and this was seen as a Godsend because we had just had a conservatory built plus the Lottery money paid for the finishing touches such as block pavement and tiles for the conservatory floor.

A few months after we had moved in I invited my clairvoyant friend Barbara round to see the new house. We decide to sit in the conservatory because it was such a lovely evening. During our conversation I stopped talking because I could hear bells ringing. Just as I was about to ask Barbara if she could her them too she turned to me and said you have a gentleman who walks around this property from the spirit world. Almost on cue a loud ringing of bells made us both jump up and I opened up the conservatory door and we listened; nothing. But once the door was closed we heard it again. In fact, since that particular evening I have heard the ringing bells again. In addition, sometimes when you sit in our conservatory you can hear sounds like a train approaching. Both Howard and I have experienced it. Yet if we hear it and ask someone to listen for the noise it does not happen. Spooky thing is many years ago the neighbouring village of Welton used to have a station and so did Daventry plus where the new houses have been built a railway line would have been constructed to serve both railway stations. So was it the wind or were we hearing a ghost train?

As each day goes by I become further devoted to this property because this house welcomes not only human beings or pets but a large amount of spiritual energies. Not long after we moved in I had the strangest dream or vision because I was standing in the background about to enter the house when a man came out of the kitchen dressed in long robes. He had a weird-looking eye as if it was false and a big Irish wolfhound close to his side. The man proceeded to tell me that my home was so protected that no one would ever break in or damage it and at that point he directed me to have a look over the back garden fence and when I did there were young babies representing a child from every country in the world. He continued to say I would be recognised wherever I went in the world. This was very bizarre to me and I could not take in what I had seen or heard. Also, while I had been living at this property I had become more spiritually open and sensitive to people and situations around me. For example, I worked in an office full of mainly female staff and only the one or two male members of staff. However, I honestly never felt totally comfortable working there because no matter where you went in that building it felt like you were sharing it with spirit energies from the past. Marie, one of the women who worked at the front end of the office, swore blind that she had seen a complete stranger, a female wearing a bright red coat enter the staff room. Marie was so convinced that she leapt from her desk and went into the staffroom only to find she was totally alone. I recall hearing footsteps coming up the stairs and the door would open and close behind where I actually worked but no one would be there. Yet, now and again there would be a dark shadow that would kind of hover around you but could only be seen from the corner of your eye. Most of the staff would often comment about what they thought they had seen. Another strange event happened in the staff car park. I got into my car about to leave when I felt I was being bumped into from behind. Indeed, within a split second a car passed by me and bumped into another car that was reversing. Luckily no one was hurt but again I was being foretold of a situation before it happened. Furthermore, these types of pre-warnings started to become more apparent around me because I never acknowledged the signs in the past. Now I try to decipher them plus avoid unnecessary situations if I can. Word began to spread around the office and warehouse of my special gift and it was not long before my mobile and home telephone number would be ringing in an overactive way.

It did not take me long to make our conservatory into a spiritual little sanctuary with items such as various healing crystals, pictures of North American Indians and angel cards. One day while I was off sick my son asked if I would be interested in going to a psychic fair in the neighbouring village. Neither of us had ever been to this type of event so we went. Going to the psychic fair changed my life completely because I had a reading which consisted of tarot cards and psychometry which means holding an item that purely belongs to me and reading the vibes of past, present and the future. The information from the reading was unbelievable as messages from beyond the grave from both of my parents and

137

grandparents came through. However, the first thing the clairvoyant said to me was, 'Why are you not working for spirit full-time, you are very capable of doing so? Also, she mentioned long-distance crystal healing which I actually did a year later and became a qualified crystal healer. In addition she said the office job was going to destroy me if I remained working there. I came home reeling from the psychic reading and talked to Howard about the possibility of me leaving the office job and setting up my own business as a clairvoyant/ medium. This was the biggest decision of my life, to give up the security of a monthly paid job. My change of job was approved by Howard.

On the seventeenth of March 2002 I left the office for good and since that day I have never looked back. My spiritual vocation has grown from strength to strength. For example, I became aware of healing crystals and I must admit I was drawn towards them. I decided to research for a renowned crystal healer and I asked my angels to direct me towards the area. Funnily enough my tutor was from Belfast and like myself had been living in England a long time. The first thing he said to me was, 'Why do you want to learn crystal healing because you are a natural healer.' I was somewhat taken aback by this statement but I did complete the course. The group was split into small sections and we were asked to take part in a demonstration of the Angel Board. Each person asked the board a question and by using a glass object it would move. This was not to be mistaken for a Ouija Board because I would never get involved with such an event. The guidance and messages for everyone in the group was amazing because the information was finely detailed and none of the group could have possibly have known. Our tutor decided we should combine our spiritual energies and try table-tipping which again had some amazing results because at one point the table was being pushed between myself and a male student sitting opposite me. Instantly, I became very emotional and felt weird and eventually became totally exhausted. What I had experienced was the full-blown emotional affections of the male student; a combination of love, hate and anger. I was very surprised how quickly I had overcome the fatigued feeling but it proved to me that I could be borderline to becoming a trance medium which is someone who goes into a trance and relates information from spirit guides or loved ones who have passed over. I decided to start getting into meditating to engage closer with the spirits. As well, I sense a very strong connection to oak trees because of the previous experience down at Canada Heights and how the oak tree had protected us from unseen accidents. Therefore, I began to take notice of nature in general and the signs you can read from the clouds and direction of birds. However, the most important sign of all is that of finding white feathers because when I ask for a sign from my angels I can always guarantee I will find a snowy-white feather in my path.

It was not long before my advert was appearing in the local paper and magazines. Within the first two years of being self-employed as a clairvoyant/medium the doors of opportunity were amazing because I appeared on television and was interviewed on the local radio. The television appearance came about one evening I was browsing on the internet when I came across a website for a new lunchtime TV programme called *Loose Lips for Living TV* which is shown on Sky and stars Melinda Messenger and Richard Arnold. I don't know whether it was a voice or thought that came into my mind but I knew somehow I had to send an email to this show and my guides were insisting that I used key words. Therefore, I typed the words 'seeing fairies' plus a description of the motor-cross event at Canada Heights. Not thinking any more about the email I received a telephone call the following day from the TV show's researcher. I could not believe that I was being taken seriously. The researcher began to ask me various questions such as, about how old was I when I started to see and hear spirits? During the telephone conversation I began to pick up snippets of information from my spirit guides about the TV studios and the people involved with the show. A date was arranged for me and my husband to travel down to London and we would be met and taken to the studios. I was booked in for the first of May, a portentous date. Both TV presenters were enlightened by my experience and after the show Melinda Messenger asked if she could have a personal reading. In a way it was very strange because I had actually brought a set of tarot cards with me plus healing crystals. After my reading with Melinda I was approached by the researcher who had originally booked me for the show and asked if I would do a further five readings for various members of the TV production team. I predicted that a member of the show would become pregnant and within a short space of time Melinda announced she was having a baby.

My involvement with local radio once again stemmed from the internet and my spirit guides directing me because I was arranging to take part in a steam rally and I had the idea of inviting the male radio presenters for a reading as they tended to make fun of mediums. As a result, I had a telephone call from Jagger and Woody during their radio show inviting me to join them, which I accepted. I must admit I was feeling very scared because these two radio DJs are very clever at ripping apart their interviewees. Prior to the radio show I pulled up their pictures on the internet and printed them off. I sat down and began to study each photo separately and I wrote down snippets of information and I emailed this over to them. On the day of the interview when they both met me they could not get over how much personal information I was able to pick up by just concentrating on looking at their photographs. During the interview I had just commented that in some cases electrical appliances play up when I am around. Almost on cue their computer crashed and it had not long been installed with all the latest technology. At this point I got offered the chance of looking around the radio station and boy, was I in my element. There were so many hot spots of badly behaved spiritual activity around the building.

Before the interview was over Jagger and Woody were surprised by the outcome of my visit because both of them were sceptics and now they had proof. Even after that particular interview both DJs and their boss had a strange experience on a flight of stairs at the radio station where I had originally picked up the spiritual energy of a woman. The radio crew rang me and asked if we could do a telephone interview because they had experienced spiritual happenings. If spirit wants us to meet certain people or put us in situations it will do so.

Living in this property I began to notice a great change in the way I presented my readings and how they were received by my clients, the emotional side of when you receive a message from loved ones who had passed over because you touch on so many issues which the client can connect to.

I recall taking part in a public demonstration at one of the pubs near where I live and there were some very tough-looking blokes covered in tattoos and piercings who openly displayed their feelings at the end of their readings with tears trickling down their cheeks. This showed that even the toughest person can believe in the spirit world.

My home gives me the comfort and support to carry on with my work and I shall always be grateful to whom or whatever introduced us to Harrow Lane. I remember the first foreign holiday Howard and I had taken since we moved to the new home. We had chosen Crete because neither of us had ever been there before. Like I mentioned before, spirit will bring people into your pathway for whatever reason and this is a prime example. Howard and I had taken a local taxi into the nearest town for a spot of sightseeing and shopping plus a chance to look at the different cultures that have dissimilar traditions from us. While we were browsing in a shop I noticed a wall plaque which was renowned as the 'Third Eye'. It was shaped like an eye with a background of a beautiful colour of blue but moulded in a circle. I looked at the price but I could not justify paying that amount even though I had never seen one that large in size before. So I left the shop feeling slightly disappointed. That evening back at the resort we were trying to decide which restaurant to eat in when suddenly it felt like someone was pushing me towards the direction of an open-air family-owned restaurant. Once we sat in the restaurant I sensed that I had some spiritual business to do here even though I was on holiday. Before I knew it spirit had me giving messages and guidance to the family members of the restaurant. However, not speaking any Greek spirit assisted by placing a family friend who could speak English so spirit can break through any barrier so information can be given or received. For the remainder of our holiday we would always use the family restaurant for our evening meals as it felt like we had become part of an extended family. On our last evening before we flew back to England the owners of the restaurant had created a party-type atmosphere by bringing personal items from their home to decorate our table. Towards the end of the evening the owner, his wife, family members and staff gathered around our table. As they spoke in broken English they presented us with gifts. I was astonished to find one of the gifts was the large Third Eye that I had seen earlier in the week. It was as if spirit was saying you have been rewarded for all your hard work. I personally could not get over it. This situation can be classed as a psychic whisper when you see or hear something and somehow it will enter into your pathway at a later date. Returning to Harrow Lane, the moment I opened the front door and stepped into the hallway I really did feel physically as if something had wrapped their arms

142

around me welcoming me home. However, sometimes when we are trying to do things too quickly or too soon spirit will find a way to slow us down to do what I call a stocktake of what you have or would like to achieve in your life-path. I can give you two very good examples which happened to me both a year apart and strangely enough around similar times. Firstly, while I was studying to become a crystal healer I had a worrying issue that the mirena coil which was surgically placed in my body may have dislodged itself without me knowing. The only way to check it out was to have a scan done. However, come the day of the scan I was not prepared for what had taken place which showed the coil was still in place but there was a dark shadow of about two and half inches in dimension, the same size as a satsuma. Therefore, another scan plus blood tests were arranged but I could not sum up just exactly how I was feeling. I had to be brave not only for my husband and son but this had taken place around the Christmas season and I would be going back to the hospital in the New Year for the tests and results. All through this uncertain period I kept my faith in my guardian angels and used crystal healing on myself. I would visualise the dark shadow as a grape suddenly shrivelling up becoming dry enough to crumble with my fingers. I proceeded to go through this process right up to the moment of the scan. During the second scan I was asked if I would agree to the use of an internal camera and I gave my consent. The overall result not only baffled the medical staff but the consultant was speechless and said it was some sort of a miracle. Indeed, with the help of spiritual self-healing, angels and working very closely with the healing crystals I had overcome an ovarian cancer scare. Since that day I decided to work for spirit in whatever form or fashion and never to allow myself to worry about life. In fact, it is like being a born again Christian because I now deal with emotions whether they are on a physical or mental level differently to that of an outsider.

The second example is about not interpreting the signs correctly. It was Christmas Eve morning and Howard had just returned from working a night shift and part of me wanted to stay in bed but I decided otherwise and disregarded what my intuition was telling me. As I was leaving the house I noticed that the big inflatable snowman that stood so proudly outside the front door must have developed a slow puncture and what was left was a pathetic pile of plastic. Then I thought what else can happen? Also I realised I had put my watch on upside down and again my instinct was telling me it is not necessary to go into Daventry, but I ignored the signs. After I had finished shopping on the way back to the car park I stopped by a certain shop. I cannot explain the reason why but I get such bad vibes there. Against my better judgement I went in browsed around and then left feeling very strange and peculiar. Suddenly I had visions of being pushed from behind which I did not like. I got into my car and as I was leaving the car park a woman in an oncoming car who did not see me came crashing into my car. It was then that I realised I had completely blocked out all the important signs which were telling me to stay at home and not go into town. Since that day I do not ignore any of the signs that spirit gives me. For example, I began to have sensations of being followed around my house by a strange male spirit energy and it got to the point were I called out, 'Whoever you are give me a name.' Later that evening I heard a gentleman's voice telling me his name was Fritz and that he was married but his wife died a tragic death. I felt heat and a huge flash as he spoke about her plus he had a son whose name began with H. Also I could actually see Fritz, his little neat beard and curly hair and his trimmed clothes displaying he was of a higher class. I went onto the internet to check my emails but my thoughts were interrupted by Fritz and immediately I was typing in the name Fritz but I never expected to find an answer – or did I? I found a full biography of Fritz Haber. Furthermore, as I read the information I could not get over what I was seeing in front of me because Fritz was a young chemist who had won the Nobel Prize for chemistry in 1918. Later he married and had a son called Hermann. However, over a period of time he had developed a nerve gas that would drive out the enemy and this was used in World War I. This led to a huge argument between Fritz and his wife who was also a chemist. She denounced his work and this led her to commit suicide. As I was trying to take in what I was reading I found myself thinking back to my very first spiritual experience of a young soldier who was shot in the trenches in World War I. My God, what a strange connection, why was spirit doing this to me? Being a clairvoyant/medium I am in a position where I can clearly see and hear the spirits, I am able to sense and feel spirit and know information about the spirit communicator. Usually people are just one or the other but I have been born with this wonderful gift of foreseeing the future and I would never abuse it. My spiritual life-path has taken me to various places on a local level, such as psychic fairs and my once a month event as the resident psychic for one of the local pubs where some amazing results about worldwide happenings have been foreseen and happened within a matter of days. Firstly, there was the London bombing on the 7 July 2005. I could not understand why I was being shown Liverpool and Arsenal football colours plus a bright red double-decker bus. Unknown to me I had picked up on Arsenal being the London connection and Liverpool was the name of the underground tube station that was targeted. The bus was where a device had gone off which was previously meant for another tube station. On the evening of the London bombing while I was sitting in my lounge sending out affirmations to all the innocent victims who lost their lives or were badly injured my attention was suddenly drawn towards my hallway. I could hear tapping coming from my front door and I could see the desperate

145

images of trepidation on the defenceless victims. Those images I shall take to my grave. On the second occasion I was reading for a girl and I suddenly had a vision of Harvey Nicholls, the posh shop down in London. Therefore, I gave out this information and told the girl to question it. Then I heard on the national news that a shooting had taken place at the famous store Harvey Nicholls and a shop assistant had been shot dead. I could not believe it. I have never asked spirit to show me worldwide events but it looks like my guides are assisting me in this direction. Yet, when you get a vision or sense strange information who can you tell because no one would believe you or you would be classed as a crackpot. This is why I feel very sad foreseeing future world happenings and I have not got the power to stop them from happening. My work has also taken me to beyond the United Kingdom to Dublin, Cork and Spain helping and guiding people with their spiritual needs of contacting loved ones. Also seeing people's auras can be fascinating because an aura usually means a warm bright glow around people who are of an unusual psychic sensitivity. Since I began to see auras it assists me in how that person might be feeling.

The work of a psychic can be challenging but this is what I really enjoy about all the unknown territories. For example, I was asked to do two separate ghost investigations with amazing results of communicating with spirits from the past, reliving and sensing what went before present-day events. However, the lay person does not understand how powerful remote viewing can be. Remote viewing means seeing or sensing an area before you have even been there. Receiving information this way can give you a real boost. My husband says I could be worth a fortune with my skills and knowledge in the right hands but I would never sell myself like that because I am special. This terminology special was a title that my spirit guide gave me at the age of four because I knew that I was naturally gifted but in what area I did not know. Since that day I have never looked back. Demonstrating my gift helps people from all walks of life giving proven evidence of a loved one who has passed over to the spirit world or assisting people to manifest future changes.

One morning I had taken my dog Pennie out for her usual walk. We fed the moor hens with leftovers from breakfast and I decided to walk past my favourite spot. This particular area is separated by a natural brook and beyond it lies a small area of woodland with huge oak trees plus shrubs and the wildlife is fantastic. Pennie and I stopped to watch a rabbit searching around for food when it realised we were there and popped down into its warren. Listening to the birds singing their amazing songs the whole scenario reminded me of viewing a giant television screen but no two channels are the same. This is why I will always thank spirit for guiding me towards a home that has very special and beautiful surroundings to help and assist me with my special chosen life-path. Who knows maybe I could have another dream or vision of a future new home but until that happens I am very satisfied living in Kathbern House.

20

My Spiritual House

My spiritual house is about my inner energy that flows within me. I see my body as the spiritual temple, a sacred place for me to acknowledge and develop my psychic powers to become more in tune working with spirit energies on the various levels such as clairvoyance or mediumship.

A spiritual energy field that surrounds our bodies is called an aura, which protects us and lets us know if someone oversteps into our personal space whether it is mental or on a physical level. Therefore, to protect my spiritual house I always surround my body in a gold light and I always ask my angels to guide and protect me twenty-four-seven. Also, I ground myself by visualising roots coming from my toes and from the base of my spine growing towards the earth and spreading all over the universe and personally I use the colour red as a cloak to protect me from any unknown energies that could harm me. I proceed to perform this ritual every morning without fail. At the end of the day I use a similar ritual to close down my psychic energies. In bed I visualise a black sleeping bag and step inside and zip it up saying, 'Go back to the light and thank you for coming. I need a good night's sleep.'

Psychic experiences are channelled through our five physical senses but the sixth sense is the all-important one because it extends beyond our material world, thus helping me to see both the past and the future.

Once I became more spiritually aware I would apply it to everyday situations to help family and friends because I cannot ignore the inner voice within me.

However, before I do readings I will do an opening up and closing down ritual because I have to protect my spiritual home at all times. By listening to my inner voice I can trust my intuition and wisdom to assist me in making sense of my past, present and future life-path. After all I am the keeper of this wonderful spiritual property.